C A L G A R Y

1884 ONWARD 1894

AN OFFICIAL GIFT OF THE HOST CITY
OF THE XV OLYMPIC WINTER GAMES

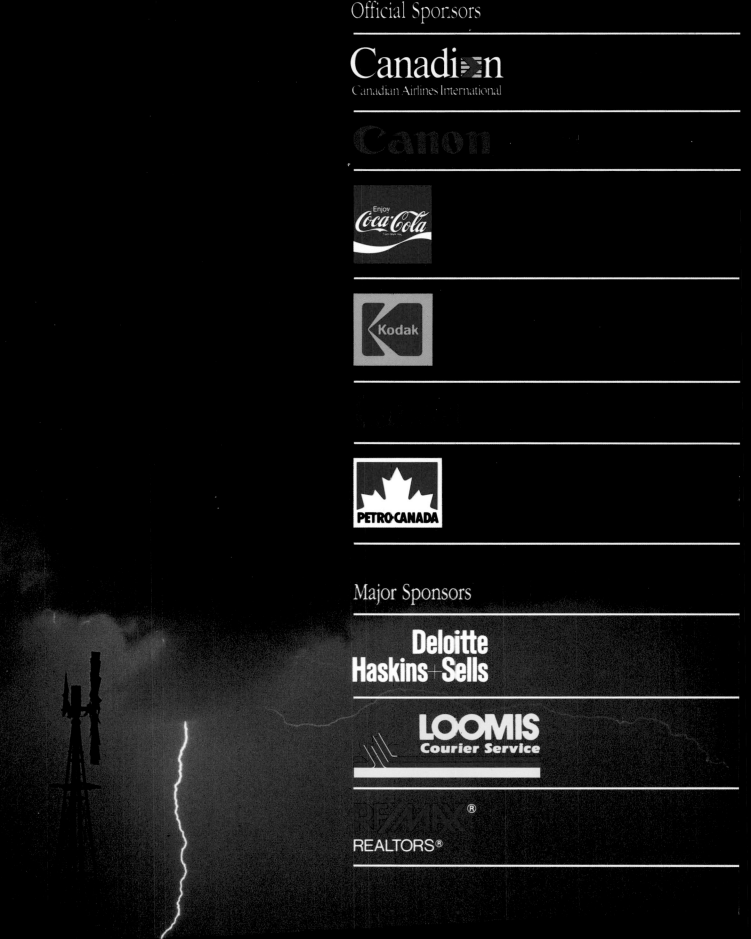

Official Sponsors

Canadian

Canadian Airlines International

Canon

Enjoy
Coca-Cola

Kodak

PETRO-CANADA

Major Sponsors

**Deloitte
Haskins+Sells**

LOOMIS
Courier Service

RE/MAX ®
REALTORS®

Major Suppliers

CLAUDIO'S BAR & BISTRO

■ Western Corporate Business Centre
○

THE WESTIN HOTEL
Calgary

The Macintosh Business Centre was honoured to play a part in "Calgary - A Year In Focus". It is the first publication of this magnitude to have been created on the Apple Macintosh computer in Canada. Accuracy combined with flexibility were maintained with the use of the Macintosh SE, Quark "XPRESS" software, and the Adobe Type Library. The Macintosh Business Centre has provided First Western Printing with the most advanced form of camera-ready artwork in the industry.

Few organizations can look back on such a rich tradition and history as Linotype. Their outstanding international reputation comes to mind whenever people think of high-quality electronic text and image processing. Linotype provides the printers and publishers of the world with the best in composition and imagesetting technology. Their contribution of a Linotronic 300 laser imagesetter to the "Year In Focus" production team is a true demonstration of Linotype's commitment to the graphic arts industry.

United Graphic Services

It has been a pleasure for United Graphics to work with the dedicated team at A Year In Focus in bringing this project to completion. The spectacular images chosen for the book were scanned on our Crosfield electronic laser equipment and then carefully organized by our page assembly specialists. "Calgary - A Year In Focus" highlights the uniqueness of this part of the country and as such, is a source of pride for everyone involved with its production.

First Western Printing

First Western Printing is pleased to have been chosen as the printer for "Calgary - A Year In Focus". The printing process is complicated and demanding, and requires the mixture of "state of the art technology" with 'old world' craftsmanship. We take extra care with all of our clients, but we are especially proud of the city of Calgary, and the book that bears its name.

Copyright ©
A Year In Focus Productions Inc.
503 - 610 Jervis St.
Vancouver, B.C. Canada
V6E 3M4

Published by:
I-Media Productions Inc.
503 - 610 Jervis St.
Vancouver, B.C. Canada
V6E 3M4
(604) 662-7687

A YEAR IN FOCUS
Executive Producer: Patrick Parenteau
Director of Marketing: Ken Brooks
Designer: Scott White
Managing Editor: Theresa Goulet

TEXT WRITTEN BY: WAYNE LYNCH
Canadian Cataloguing in Publication Data

Lynch, Wayne.
    Calgary: a year in focus
ISBN O 9693244-0-5
1. Calgary (Alta.) - Description - Views. I.
Title.
FC 3697.37.L95 1987 971.23'3 C88-091034-89
F1079.5.C35L95 1987

Designed, printed and bound in Canada.

SECOND PRINTING FEBRUARY 1988

KEVEN DALMAN

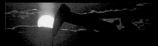

THE
BEGINNING
A YEAR IN FOCUS

"No matter how slow the film,
Spirit always stands still long enough
for the photographer It has chosen."

– Minor White

JOHN FUJIMAGARI

651

CALGARY
6:51 AND COUNTING

It is 6:51 am. Five hundred and fifty miles above the earth, in the quiet cold of the exosphere, a LANDSAT satellite registers images of Calgary, a high-tech city rising from the amber prairie. Down in the city, the sun's rays scatter a curtain of mist that shrouds the Bow and Elbow Rivers and everywhere the streets and bridges fill with their daily ration of commuters. Along a bend in the Bow a fisherman floats a fly into a quiet eddy hoping to entice a brown or rainbow trout. This is Calgary, a city like no other, a city poised for the future.

ROBERTO DE LUNA

WELCOME to Calgary
Host City of the 1988 Olympic Winter Games

DALE HANNAFORD

ROBERTO DE LUNA

PAT PRICE

JIM CARROLL

MIKE RIDEWOOD

As the sunrises, the buildings in the city's core, like mirrors in the sky, glint copper, gold and chrome. These mountains of glass prefigure the importance of the city as a major business community. Calgary is Alberta's second largest city and the financial centre of western Canada. Not only is it the nation's headquarters for the mercurial and influential oil and natural gas industry, but it ranks as one of Canada's top centres for corporate head offices.

The city is designed for people. Currently, half the office buildings in Calgary's core are linked by Plus-15's, skyways 15 feet above the traffic. Lunchers never need their coat or hat as they navigate between buildings and along rows of shops and restaurants. In summer the lunch hour reaches a crescendo when people move outdoors to the Stephen Avenue Mall and the numerous sidewalk cafes.

DAVE PULLAR

17

KEVEN DALMAN

DAVE OLECKO

GEORGE WEBBER

KEN A. MEISNER

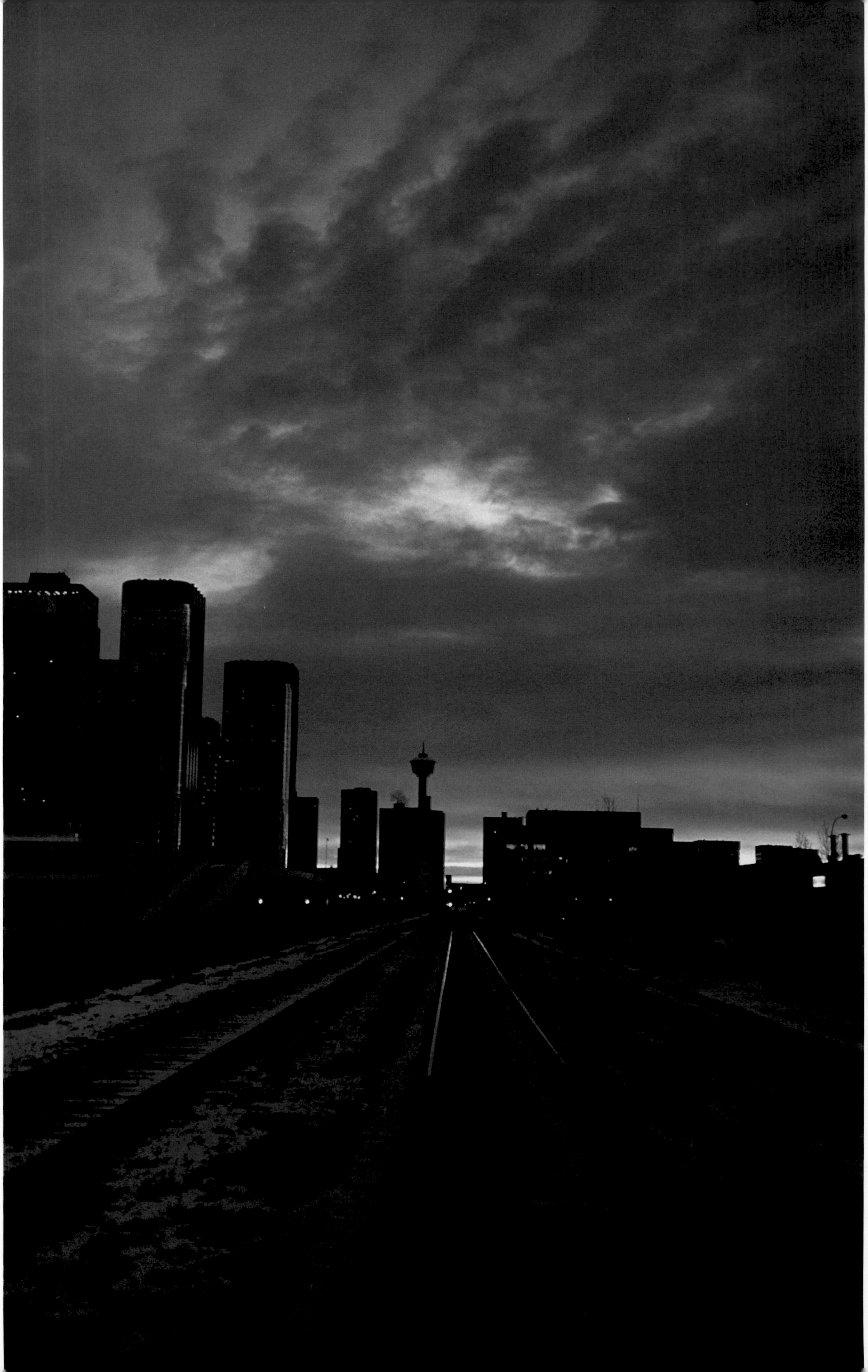

KEN A. MEISNER

GEORGE WEBBER

RICK RUDNICKI

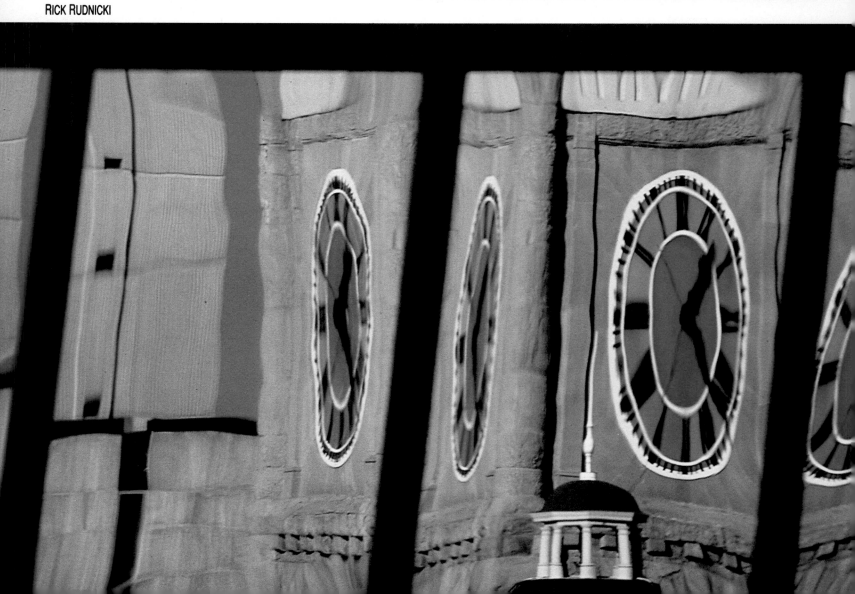

The history of Calgary began 15,000 years ago at the end of the last glaciation. As the Ice Age waned, grazing animals migrated into the area, and with them, human hunters. In the millennia that followed, the Indians hunted bison, first on foot, and then after 1750, on horseback. In 1876 the RCMP established Fort Calgary and within 10 years the railway had also arrived, a harbinger of the city's future eminence as a transportation centre. In the early years after the city's incorporation in 1884, Calgary belonged to the cattlemen. Twenty years later, however, farming spread through the prairies eating up great sections of former cattle range, and the distribution and transport of grain became a new stimulus in the growth of the city.

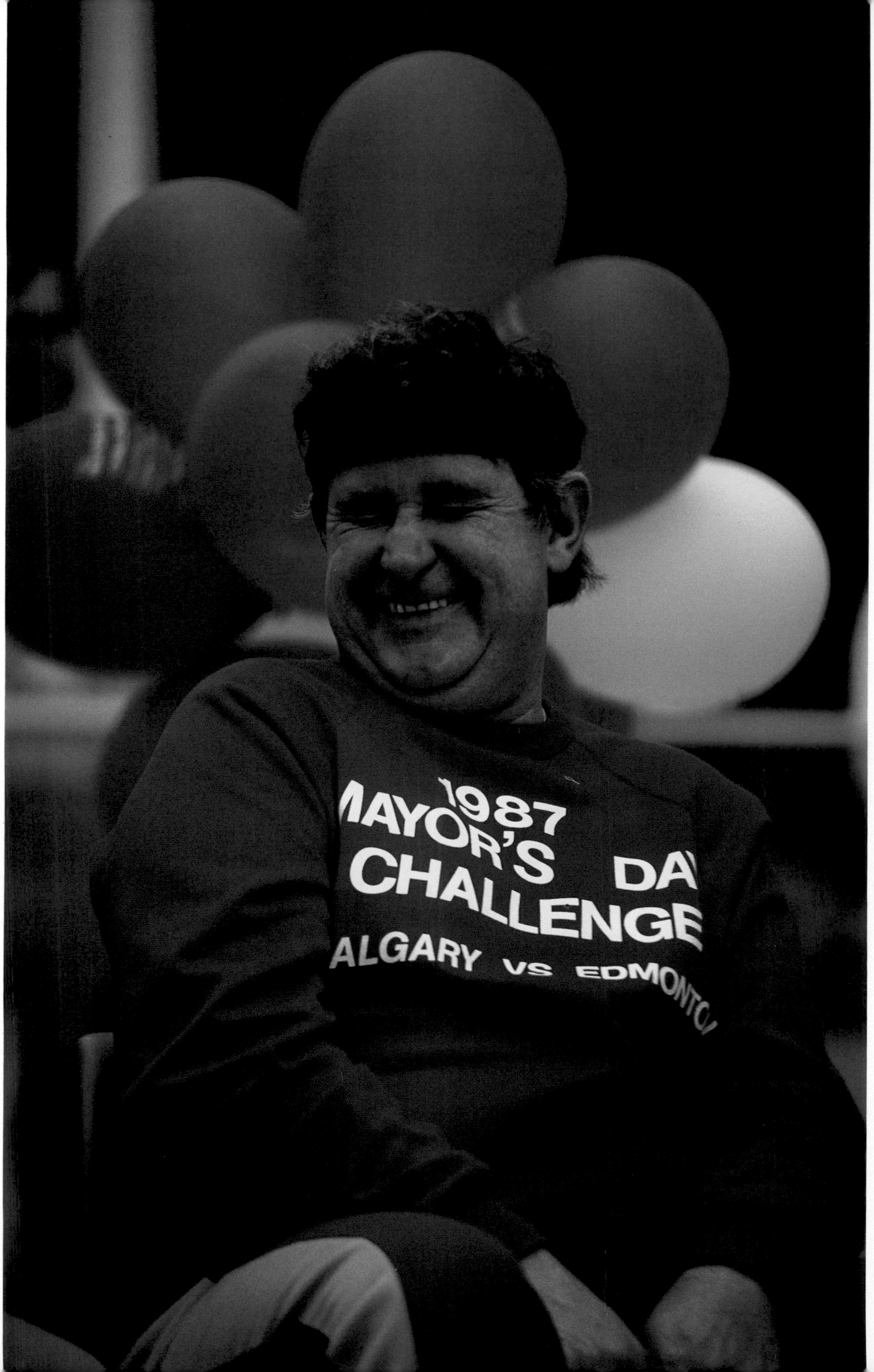

RICK RUDNICKI

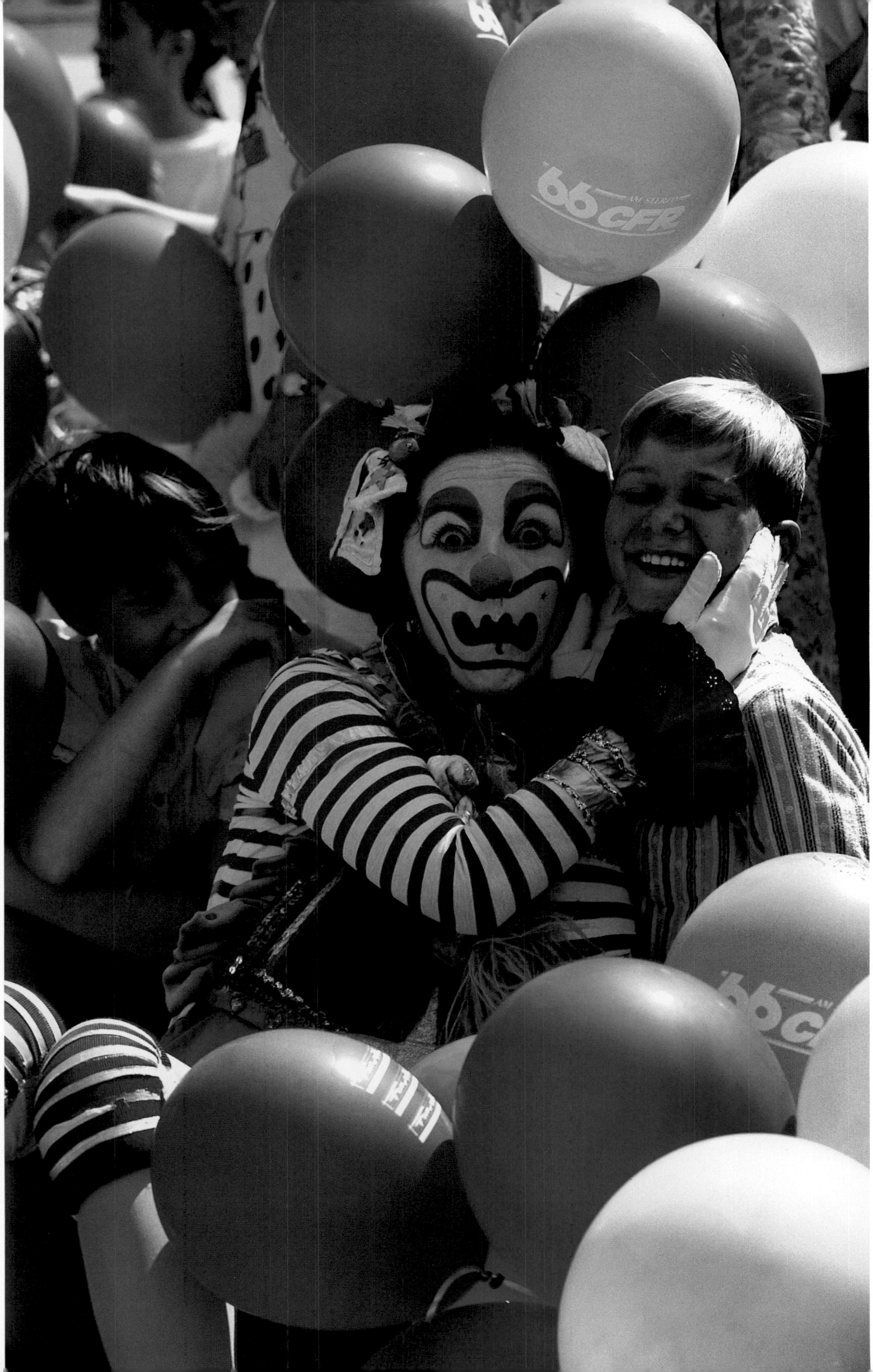

RICK RUDNICKI

Fish Creek Provincial Park spans the southern end of Calgary. The park is a lush riverine habitat rich with animal life and quiet places. Within the park can be found owls and coyotes, mink, beaver and grouse, and in occasional years black bears wander through. You don't expect to find a wildlife area such as Fish Creek in a city with 600,000 people, and yet it is only one of Calgary's many natural areas, all of which add a wilderness flavour to the urban setting.

PAT PRICE

PAT PRICE

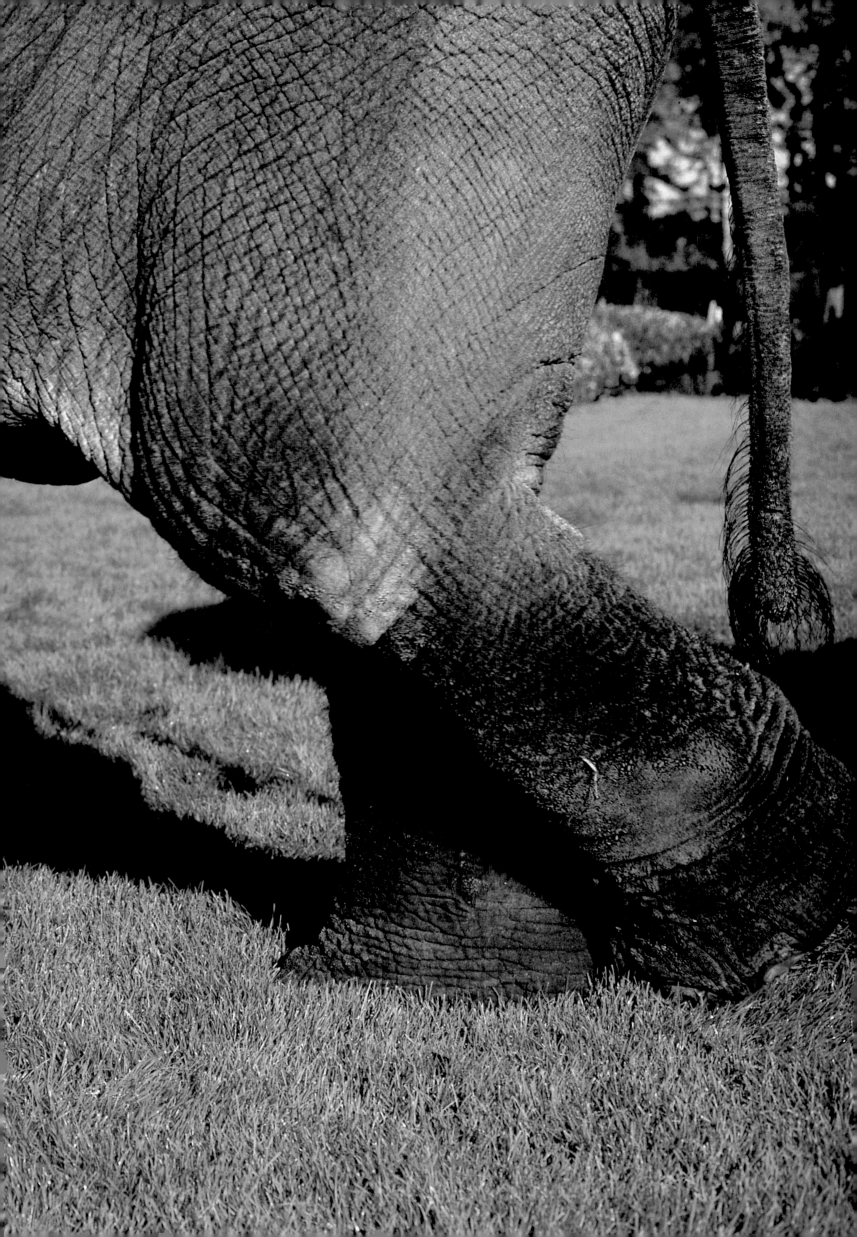

KEN A. MEISNER

MARK VITARIS

DANNY RIEDLHUBER

The most important role of the modern zoo is the breeding of endangered species, and in this respect the Calgary Zoo ranks as one of the most successful in North America. The zoo has successfully bred such reproductively temperamental species as spectacled bears, snow leopards and Asiatic elephants. It was the zoo's impressive record which finally convinced China to loan them a pair of rare giant pandas in 1988.

The most unique exhibit at the Calgary Zoo is the Prehistoric Park, a display of several dozen life-size replicas of dinosaurs and other prehistoric creatures set in a landscape of living plants and sculptured rock. When you consider the park along with the Tyrrell Museum of Paleontology in Drumheller and Dinosaur Provincial Park, (a UNESCO World Heritage Site near Brooks), it is clear that Alberta is one of the best loc-ations in the world to study dinosaurs.

WAYNE LYNCH

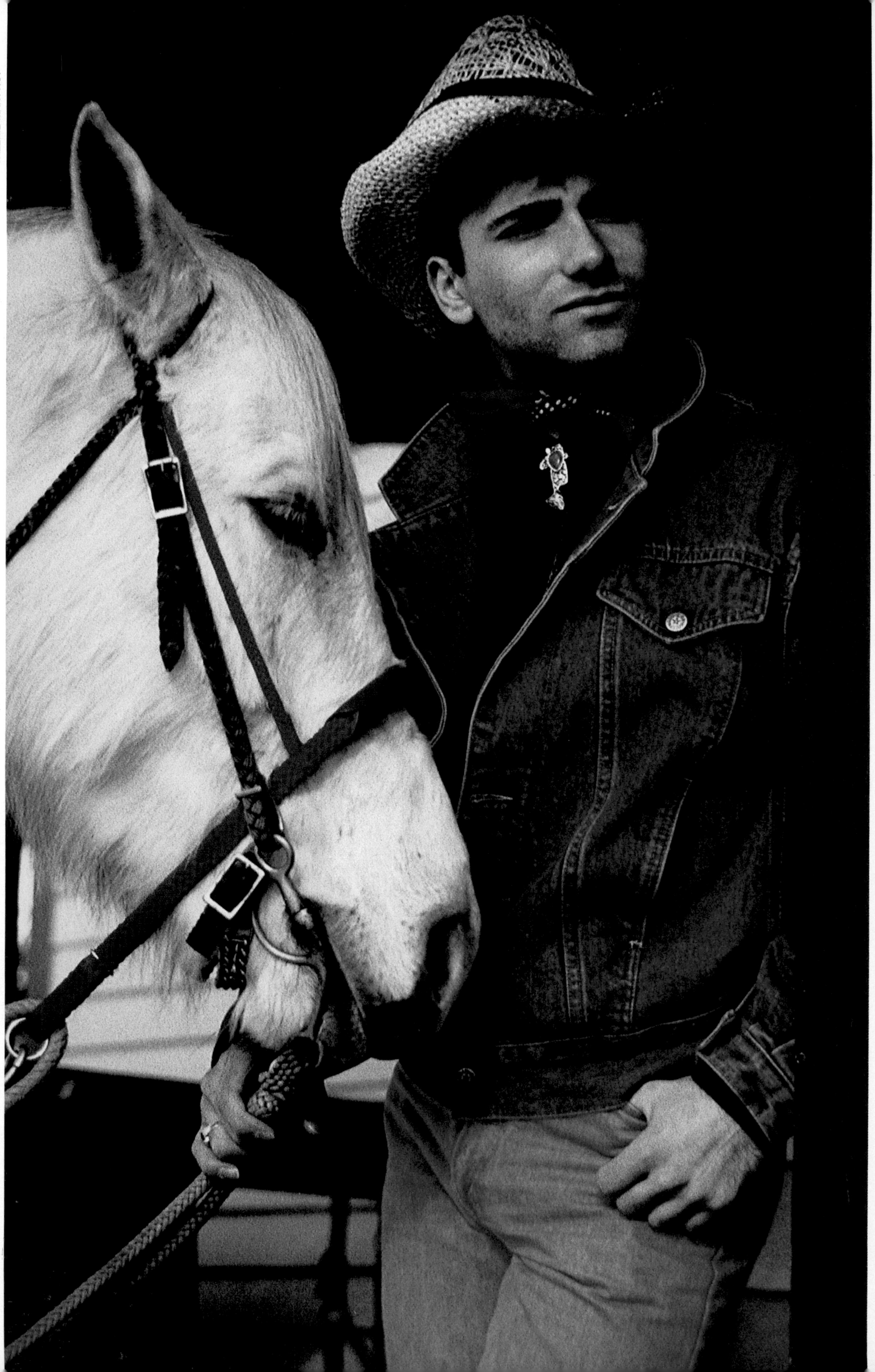

VALERIE MANTYKA

PETER HOLTON

IAN TOMLINSON

KEN A. MEISNER

IAN TOMLINSON

36

IAN TOMLINSON

IAN TOMLINSON

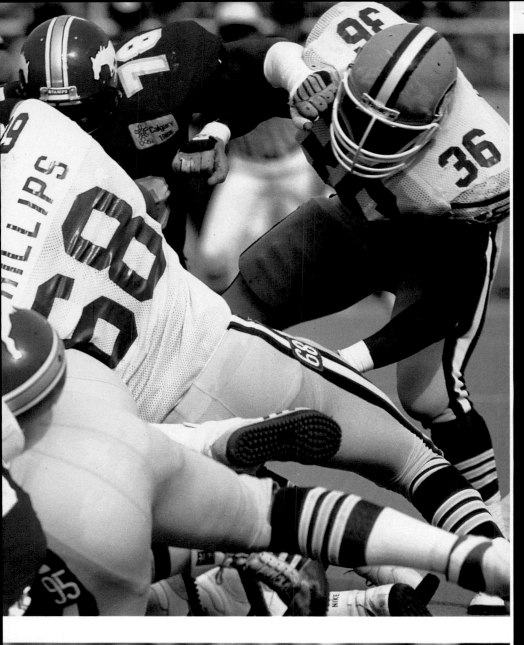

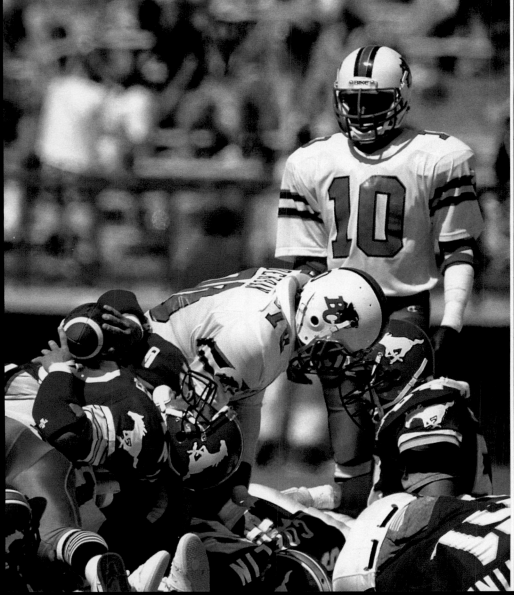

At the end of the working day the thoughts of many Calgarians turn to exercise and recreation. For cyclists and joggers there are miles of trails and paved paths that weave through wooded parks and along scenic waterways. For those who want to ride into the sunset there are a number of public riding stables. Undoubtedly the most renowned equestrian facility is Spruce Meadows, a few miles south of the city. Set amid rolling foothills and aspen woodlands, Spruce Meadows is a world-class show jumping centre that hosts international tournaments.

JIM CARROLL

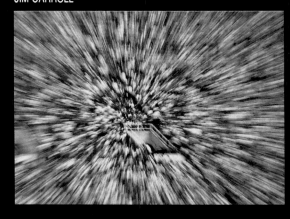

DANNY RIEDLHUBER

DANNY RIEDLHUBER

LARRY MARTINI

AL TAMBOSSO

41

IAN TOMLINSON

RICK RUDNICKI

Calgarians enjoy competition. Gymnasiums, arenas, pools and racquet clubs are found in every neighbourhood of the city and once you have exhausted your body there are numerous spectator sports to further rouse the spirit. In every season of the year you can shout from the sidelines in support of the hometown team as the Stampeders, Flames and Cannons battle respectively for the pigskin, the puck and RBI's.

IAN TOMLINSON

PAT PRICE

DAVE PARKER

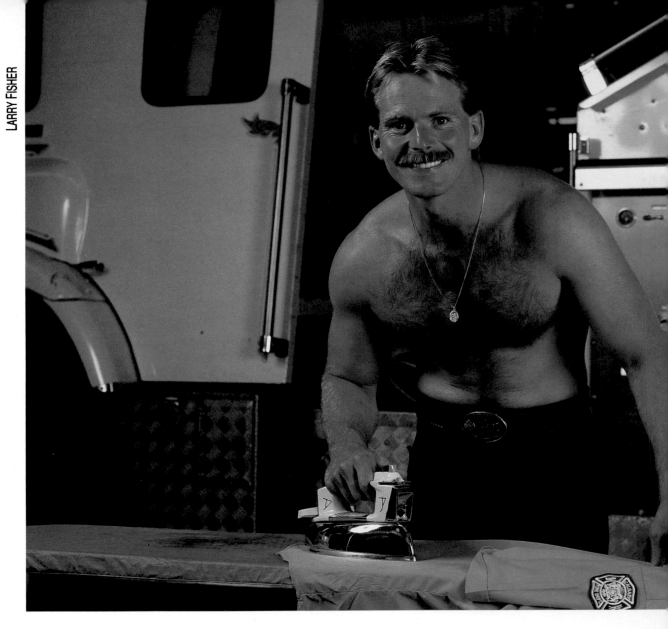

JIM CARROLL

LARRY FISHER

ALAN MERRETT

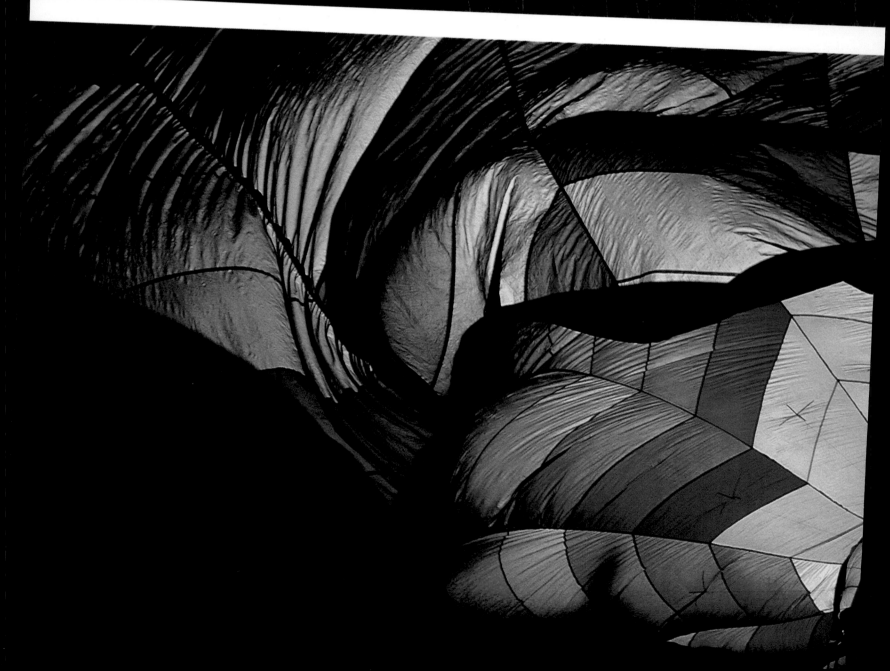

KEN A. MEISNER

The rising thermals of a prairie morning launch fleets of hot-air balloons that skim across the skyline. The colourful balloons are emblazoned with logos. But besides relaying their message of corporate prosperity, they create an atmosphere of gaiety, and their passage enlivens the moment for people commuting to work.

BRUCE PICKERING

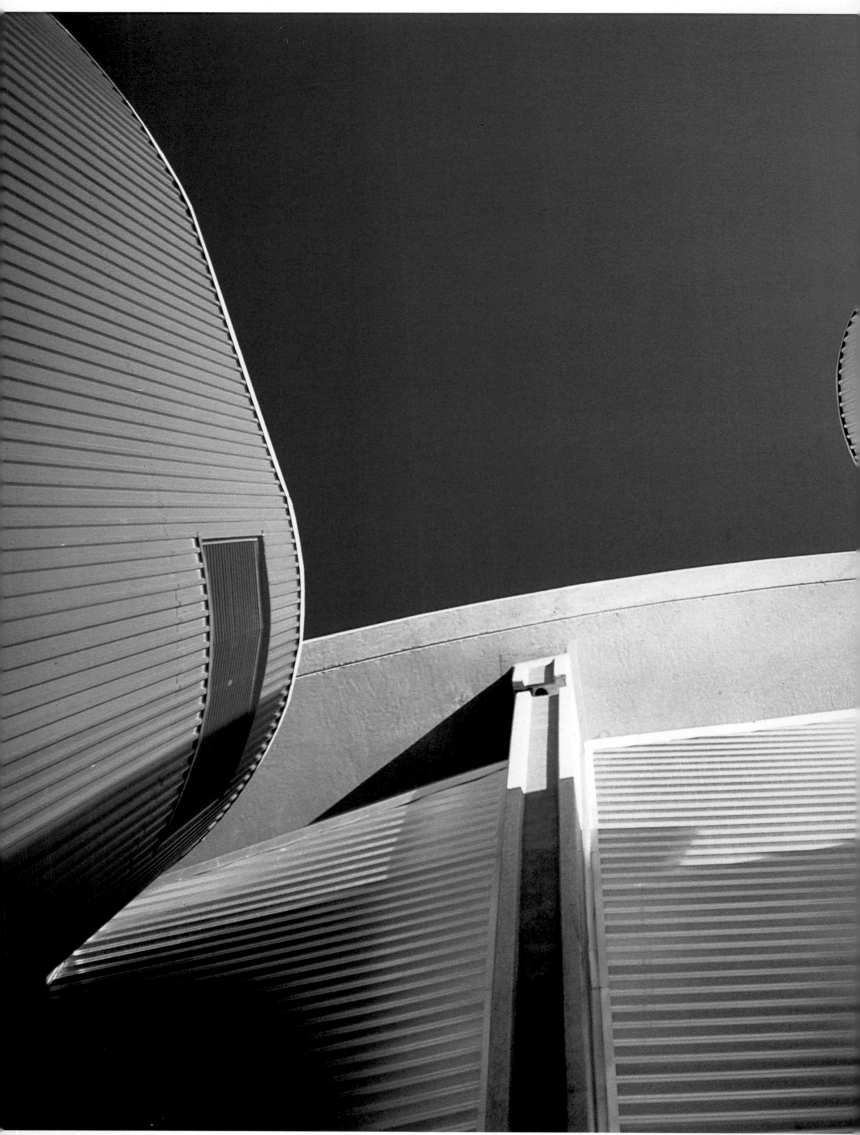

JOHN BICKNELL

266·7268

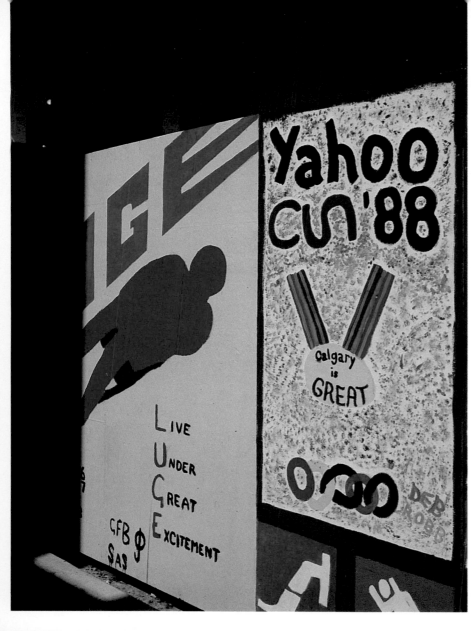

Calgary's appeal has a lot to do with its lenient attitude. The city doesn't stand on protocol when so much of protocol is anachronistic. This is a city for entrepreneurs, dreamers and schemers. Calgary is spontaneous and productive, and has developed a style based on midwestern traditions, and international flare.

GEORGE BRYBYCIN

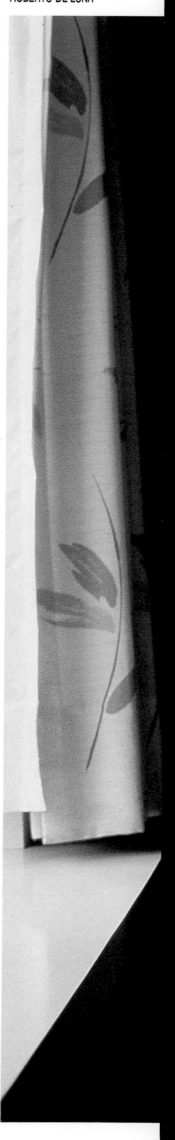

ROBERTO DE LUNA

DAVID CHIDLEY

ROBERTO DE LUNA

The city has never forgotten its past and the people who made it memorable. In Calgary's Heritage Park you can slip back in time when the clang of the blacksmith's anvil accompanied the blast from the steam engine's whistle. Authentic buildings depict pioneer life at the turn of the century and help us to remember how the West began.

DAVID CHIDLEY

The city's personality is never more visible than during the Calgary Stampede. The friendliness is palpable and the western spirit infects everyone, bankers, clerks and executives alike. Even doctors and nurses dress in western garb and liberally dispense "yahoos", the surest adjunct to speed up convalescence. In short, like the prairie itself, the people of Calgary are open and outgoing.

HANK BOERE

63

STAMPEDE
ROPERS, RIDERS & WRESTLERS

I have watched a cowboy grow. I saw him bruise, and bleed, and cry; and I saw him ride, and rope, and win, and I liked the man he became. You do not become a cowboy by wearing a stetson and fancy leather boots. The cowboy is from another time. His beliefs of today are infused with yesterday and his hope for tomorrow never falters.

DAVE OLECKO

PAT PRICE

DAVE OLECKO

PAT PRICE

The rodeo is the game that cowboys play and the Calgary Stampede is the biggest game of them all. The first Stampede was held in September 1912 and the hero that year was Tom Three Persons, a Blood Indian from MacLeod, Alberta. At the heart of every rodeo is the struggle between man and beast and Tom's opponent that year was Cyclone, a muscled stallion that was blacker than a bronc buster's bottom. The stallion had never been ridden and thousands cheered as the hometown boy showed them who was tougher.

The early rodeo had its start in the 1700's when the Spanish vaqueros brought the tradition to California, and events of daring were staged to celebrate holidays. Later, working cowboys throughout the west often broke the tedium of months on the trail with contests that demanded skill and competitive spirit. Out of these beginnings came the modern rodeo, one part contest and one part showmanship.

JERRY CLEMENT

DAVID CAROL

MIKE RIDEWOOD

MIKE RYAN

The classic rodeo event is one of the sport's oldest-saddle bronc riding. When the buzzer blares the cowboy must stay with his mount for eight to ten seconds while it spins, bucks and jerks. His only hold is a single rein and bronc riders must have coined the expression "riding by the seat of your pants". A rider spurs his mount to greater heights and twists to enhance his score, but if he loses a stirrup or touches the horse with his free hand he is "out of the money".

The most popular event with the cowboys is the bull riding, despite its reputation for danger. A bucking bull is 3/4 of a ton of irritable bovid that not only wants to dislodge the rider but also grind him into the ground for good measure. So why run the risk? One bullrider confided, "I love this sport because all it takes is brawn and no brains". He smiled and walked away.

MIKE RIDEWOOD

MIKE RYAN

DAVE PULLAR

GERARD YUNKER

DAVID CAROL

GERARD YUNKER

From above the Bow River along Centre Street you can watch the sun disappear behind a bank of buildings in the city's core. With a sweep of the eye you can see the glitter of neon and glass, the peaceful rolling foothills swathed in acres of sun-bleached wheat, and the alluring white peaks of the majestic Rockies. Why would any Calgarian ever leave home?

PAT PRICE

LARRY FISHER

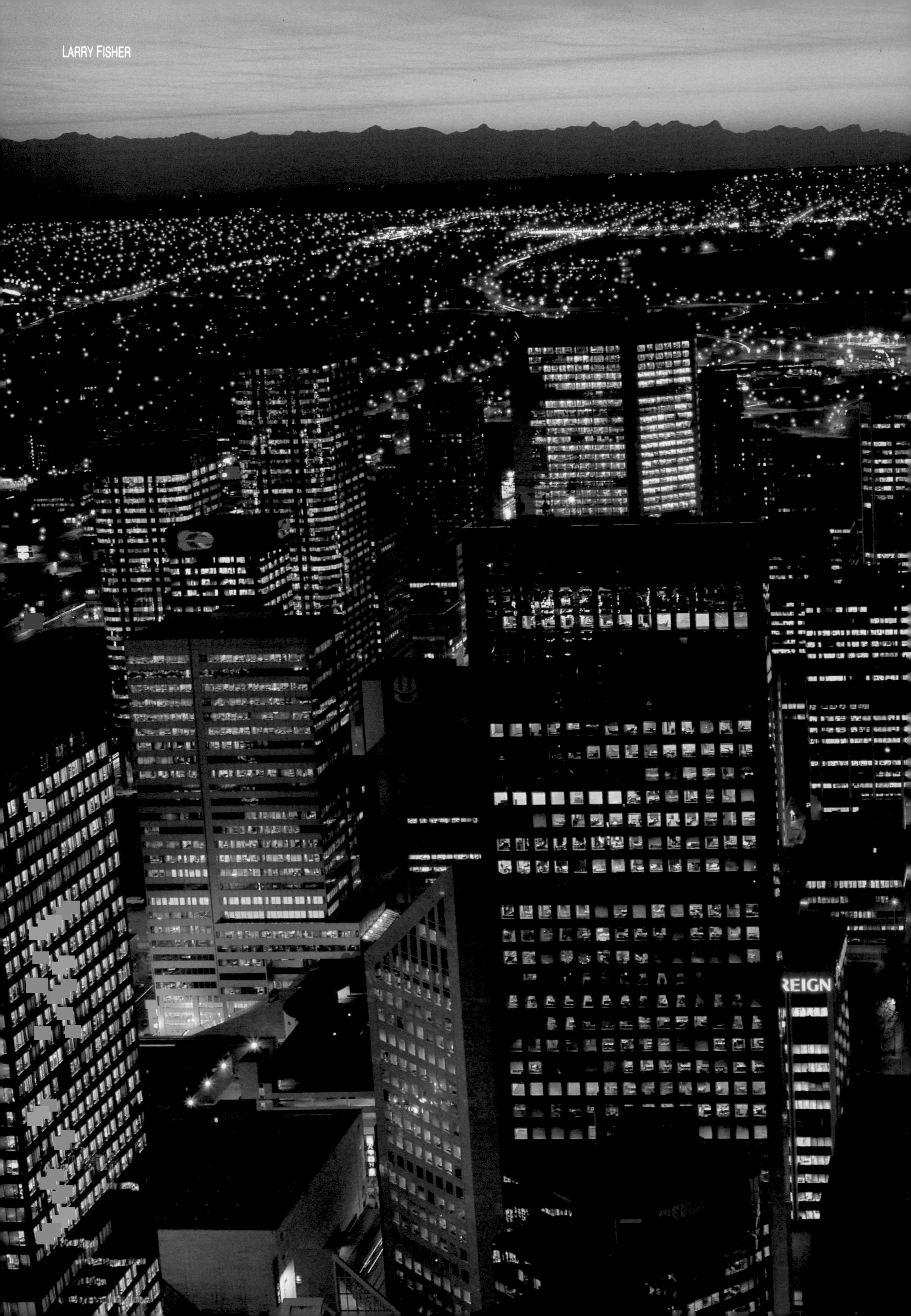

It is still believed that going out in Calgary means dining on steak and beer, and doing a circuit of local "watering holes" while you tap your boots to the lament of a western songster. Well, those times are gone along with the innocence of the sixties, and Calgary is now vibrant and varied. Calgary has grown up.

The city has many restaurants – from the unpretentious cafes which emphasize quality and presentation, to those that feature the elegance of haute cuisine. The epicure can choose between innumerable Eastern cuisines spiced with ginger, pepper and curry, and European fare flavoured with olives, garlic and onions.

Fortunately, you must search very hard to find the sour side of dining á la France where the sommelier blanches in disbelief when you err with a vintage.

ALAN MERRETT

VALERIE MANTYKA

GERARD YUNKER

GEORGE WEBBER

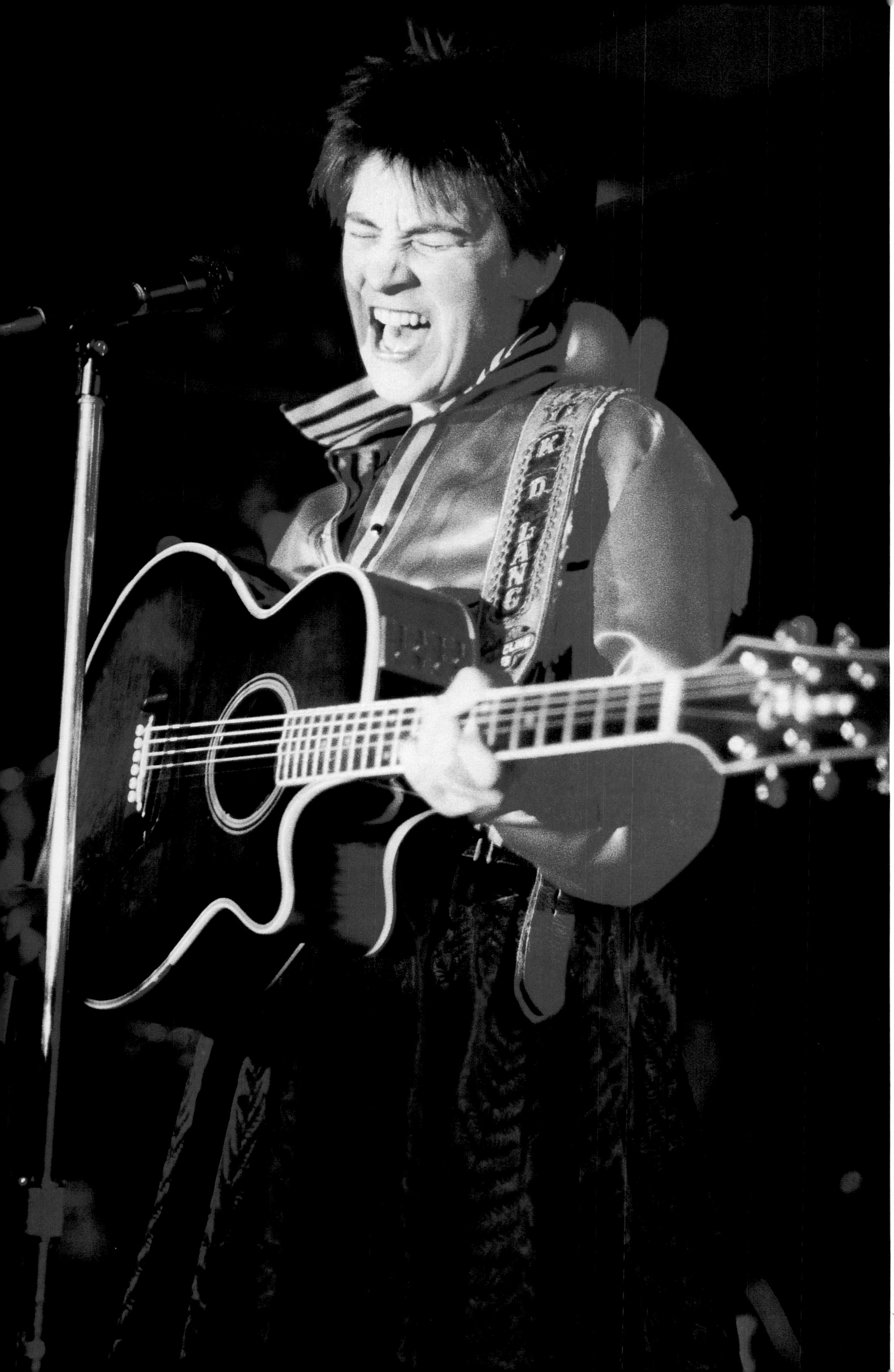

ALEXANDER THOMAS

ALEXANDER THOMAS

The art of living is not restricted to eating and Calgary at night offers much to tantalize your artistic cravings. The community's commitment to culture reached its apogee with the opening of the Centre for Performing Arts, Canada's newest most spectacular Complex of its kind. The Centre spreads over a full city block and provides the best in facilities for talents which deserve the best. Elsewhere you can enjoy dinner theatre, comedy clubs, museums and galleries, but when you want to be lost in youth you must go to Electric Avenue.

Along the strip you are immersed in pulsating rhythms, rainbows of neon and the familiar tune of ice cubes on glass. The Avenue breathes exuber-ance and typifies the atmosphere that is Calgary in the eighties: youthful, relaxed and cosmopolitan.

ALEXANDER THOMAS

GEORGE WEBBER

ROYAL BANK

DOUGLAS CURRAN

LARRY FISHER

GERARD YUNKER

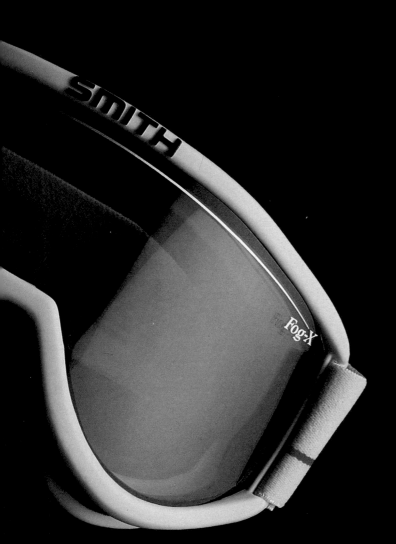

GOING FOR GOLD

THE COMPETITION BEGINS

IAN TOMLINSON

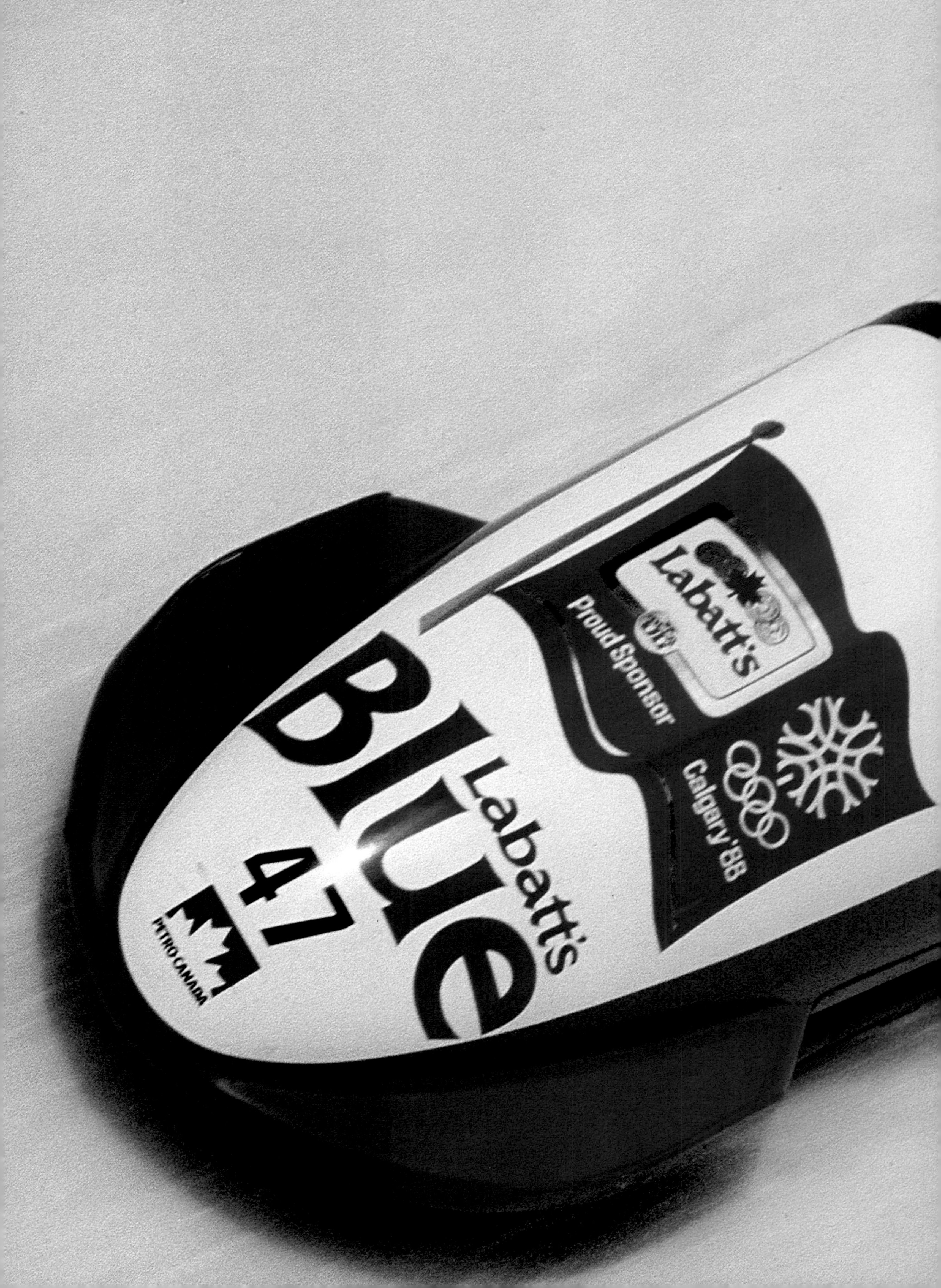

GOING FOR GOLD

THE COMPETITION BEGINS

The XV Olympic Winter Games are the most important winter sporting competitions ever held in Canada. Assembled are the best male and female athletes on earth, each burning with a passion to succeed and a desire to excel, and Canada hosts this great competition with a strength of purpose that any olympian would envy.

AL TAMBOSSO

RICK RUDNICKI

MIKE RIDEWOOD

Symbolism and tradition are a part of every spectacle and those linked with the Olympics are especially meaningful. The five interlocking rings represent the co-operation between nations and cultures in a spirit of equality and friendship. In 1988 the Olympic symbol will be joined by the host city's emblem, a stylized maple leaf. The leaf, symbolic of Canada, consists of five interlocking C's which represent the union of the continents joined together for the Olympics. And finally, the lofty aspirations of every olympian are embodied in the Olympic Motto: "Citius, Altius, Fortius", Faster, Higher, Stronger.

PAT PRICE

RICK RUDNICKI

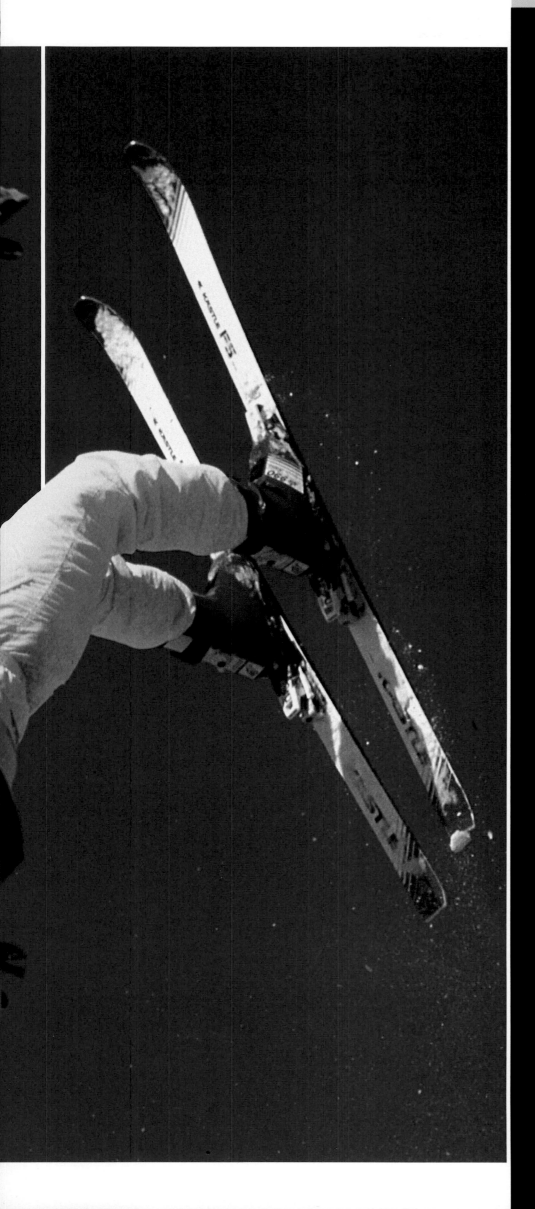

The Games were born in ancient Greece, possibly as part of harvest festivals held at the religious centre of Olympia. In the beginning, foot races were the only event and races were held every four years from 776 B.C. onwards. Gradually, the Games expanded and at their pinnacle included foot races, boxing, wrestling, chariot and horse races, and the most prestigious event of all, the pentathalon. All of the contestants were male and all were Greek citizens. The athletes competed in the nude and the victors were crowned with a wreath made from the branch of an olive tree.

MARK VITARIS

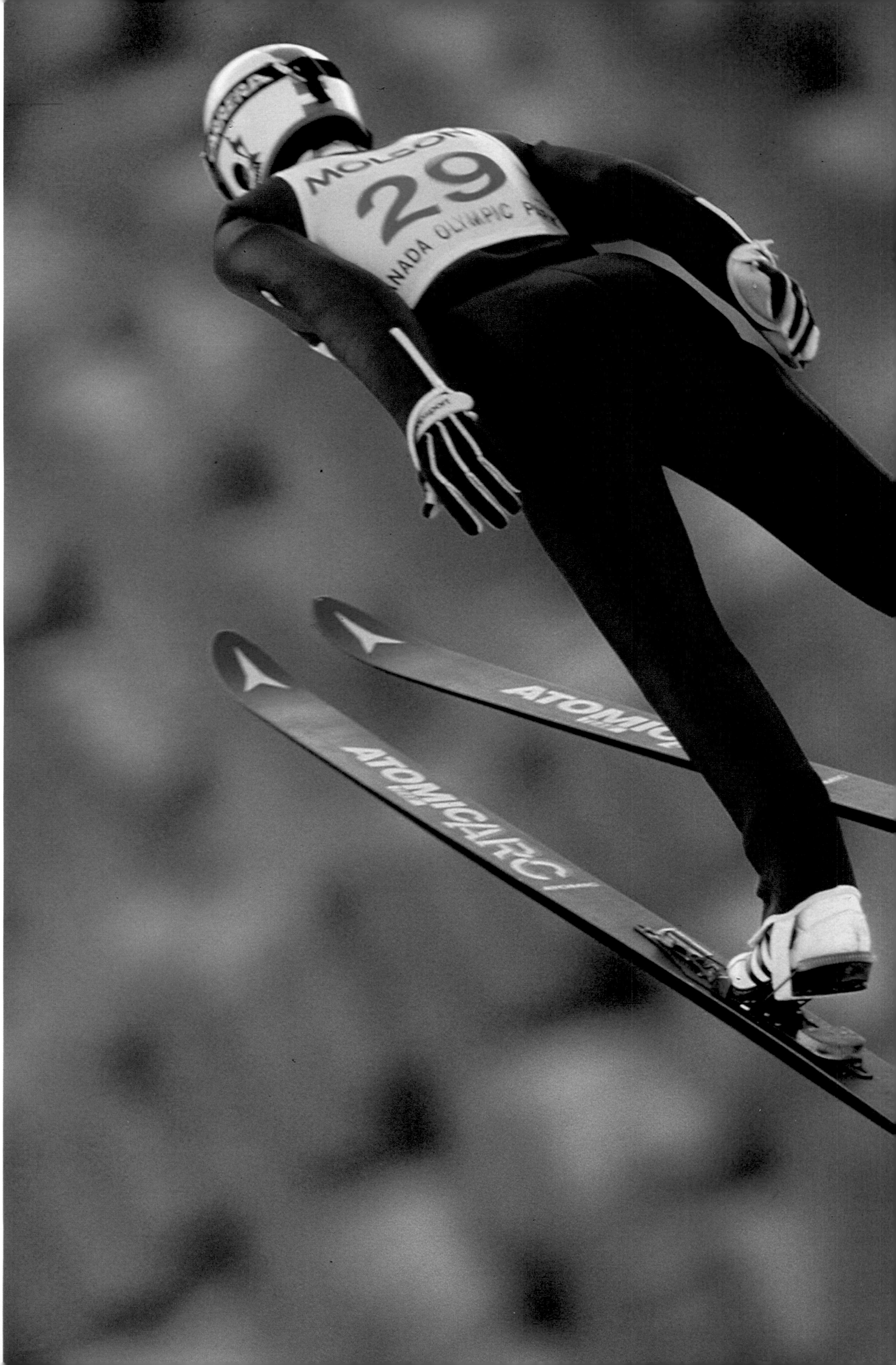

IAN TOMLINSON

Dave Pullar

Roy Sullivan

At the time, ancient Greece was often fragmented by war between its neighbouring city-states, but the Greeks felt so strongly about the importance of athletic competition that they always declared a sacred truce during the weeks that the Games were staged. The Games continued even after the Greeks were conquered by the Romans. But a Christian Roman emperor, judging the contests to be nothing more than a heathen carnival, finally abolished the Games in 394 A.D.

It took 1500 years to rekindle the Olympic competitive spirit. A French aristocrat, Baron de Coubertin, orchestrated the resurrection, and the first modern Olympic Games were held in Athens in 1896.

ROCK WHITNEY

IAN TOMLINSON

RICK RUDNICKI

McDonald

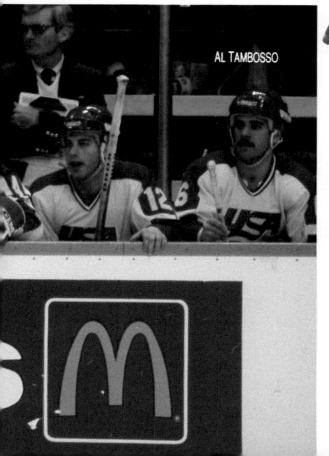

AL TAMBOSSO

DAVID CORRY

Western Airlines
he only way to fly.

NAKISKA
CP Hotels
Banff Springs

MOUTON-CADET

START
Celebrity Ski Invitational

PETER HOLTON

DOUG LEIGHTON

In the words of Baron de Coubertin, "The most important thing in the Olympic Games is not to win but to take part, just as the most important thing in life is not the triumph but the struggle. The essential thing is not to have conquered but to have fought well".

In September 1981 the official announcement was made of who would host the 1988 Olympic Winter Games. It was the culmination of 20 years of dedicated effort to bring the Olympics to Calgary. Calgarians will accrue many benefits from hosting the Olympics, the least of which will be the superlative sporting facilities and the enhancement of civic pride. But the benefits go well beyond Calgary.

DAC DANG

113

The Olympics will benefit all Canadians. Politicians stress the economic activities, employment gains, augmented tourism, and many other monetarily attractive features. The true value of the Games however, goes deeper than our wallet. The Olympics will force each of us to look beyond our national boundaries and take a closer look at the rest of the world. We will see ourselves as one of a community of nations, all of whom share a common aspiration for a better life.

In a world that so readily applauds mediocrity, the Olympic Games rewards pursuit of excellence. As a nation, our endorsement and hosting of these Games reflects our belief in the merit of this high ideal.

MIKE RYAN

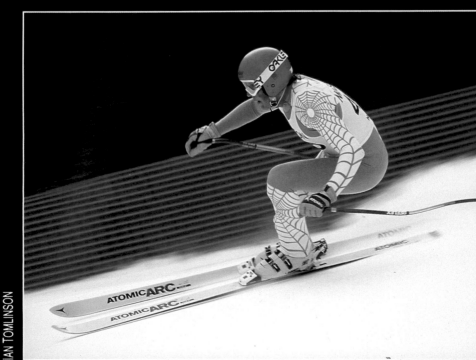

GERARD YUNKER

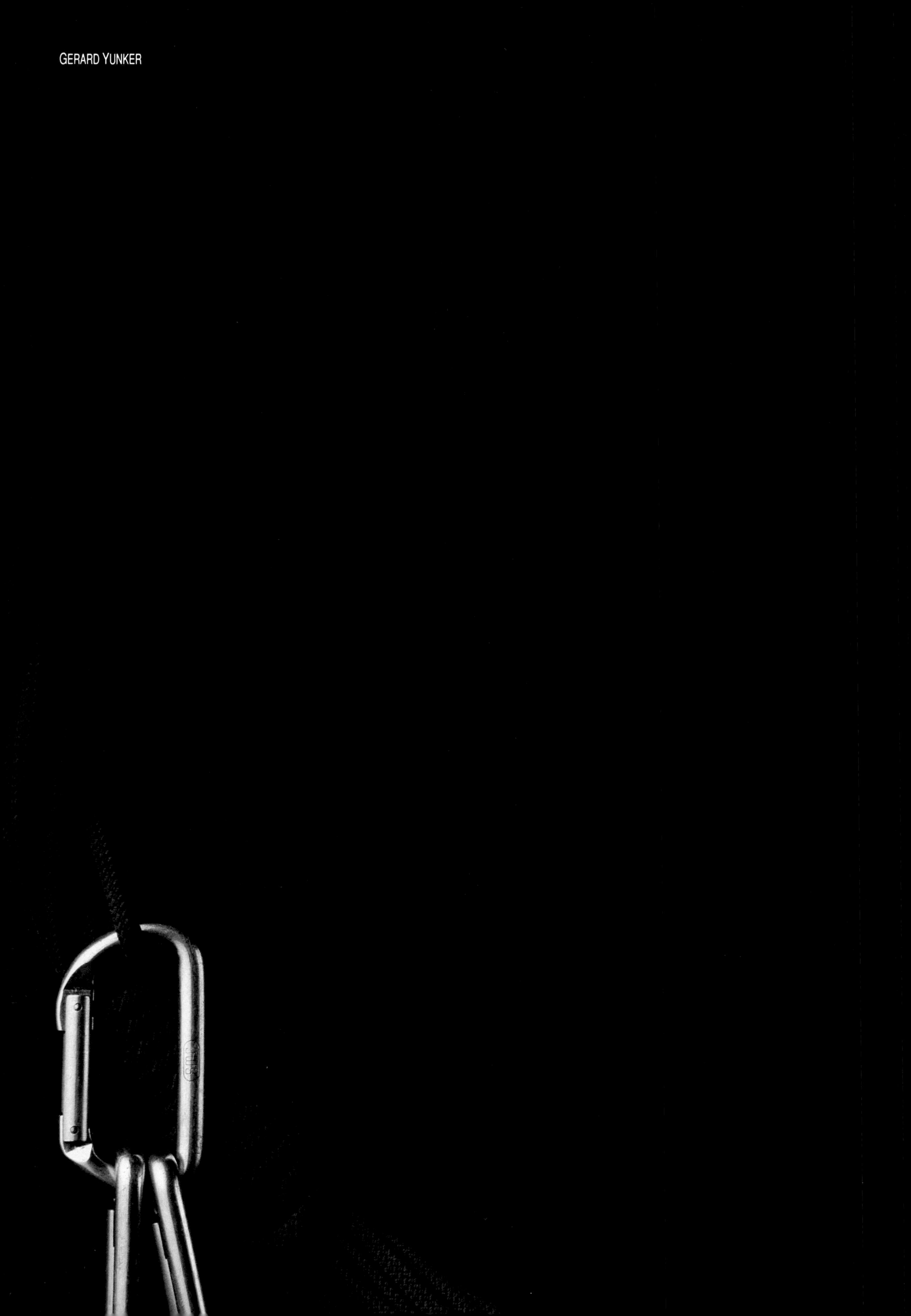

MOUNTAINS
THE FLOOR OF THE SKY

SCOTT ROWED

MOUNTAINS
THE FLOOR OF THE SKY

The Rocky Mountains are more than timbered slopes, tumbling water and naked, raw peaks. They are a land of pleasant uncertainty where the human spirit can stretch and grow. In the mountains you can discover life. In the mountains you can recapture your dreams and challenge your fears. In the mountains you can live.

The Rockies are old but not ageless. To understand the origin of the Rockies you must understand the crust of the earth and how it behaves. The earth's crust is not a continuous, solid shell of rock, but an assemblage of gigantic pieces that continually move about the surface of the earth, sliding past each other, colliding and moving apart. Eighty million years ago one of these pieces of crust, the continent of North America, collided with the crust underlying the Pacific Ocean, and, over millions of years thrust up the Rocky Mountains.

GEORGE BRYBYCIN

LARRY FISHER

As soon as mountains are born they begin to disappear, and water is the liquid leveller. Rain, sleet, raging rivers and expanding ice chip away at the lofty peaks, and particle by particle, rob them of their stature. The process is slow and continuous, 1/2" every 1000 years. The Rockies still retain the angular peaks and sharp edges of a youthful range but if you want a glimpse of what the future holds, just consider the much older Appalachian Mountains in eastern North America.

The Appalachians once had the highest peaks the earth has ever known, three miles higher than Mount Everest, and have since been whittled down to a fraction of their former size.

DOUG LEIGHTON

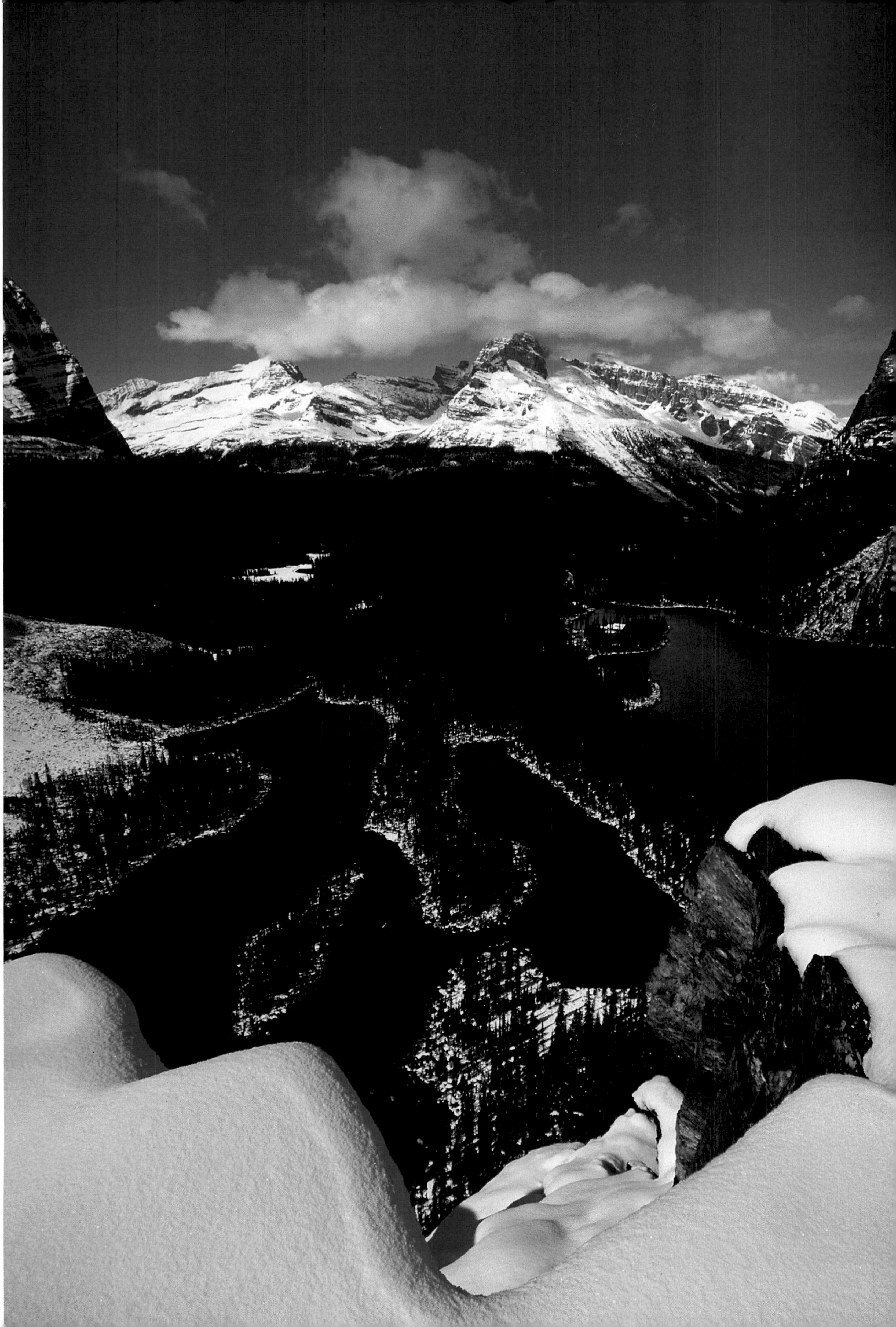

WAYNE LYNCH

LES MESZAROS

CARLOS AMAT

CARLOS AMAT

The appeal of the Rockies rests as much with their diversity as with the height of their peaks. This diversity manifests itself in the abundant wildlife, the rich plant life, and the varied landscapes. As you climb a mountain the plants and animals change. At the base of the mountain is the montane zone, a mixture of grasslands, pine and aspen forests. This zone is an essential winter feeding range for deer, elk and bighorn sheep. Higher up is the subalpine zone, between 2000 feet and the timberline at 6500 feet. This middle zone is a thick forest of spruce and fir, the home of the black bear, spruce grouse, lynx and hare. Beyond the timberline is the alpine zone, an open area of lush meadows where caribou, mountain goats and grizzlies are found.

WAYNE LYNCH

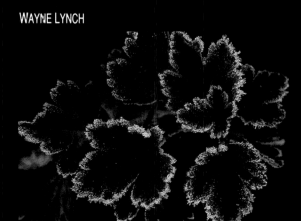

WILDLIFE
MAJESTY, MUSCLE AND GRACE

As I watched the grizzly, its nose was never still, twisting from side to side, momentarily distorting the massive face with comic affect. Its snout reached up to the warm spring air, teasing out the faint scent of ripe carrion from the background odours of nectar, sap and greenery. The bear turned and disappeared into the tangle.

KEITH LOGAN

WAYNE LYNCH

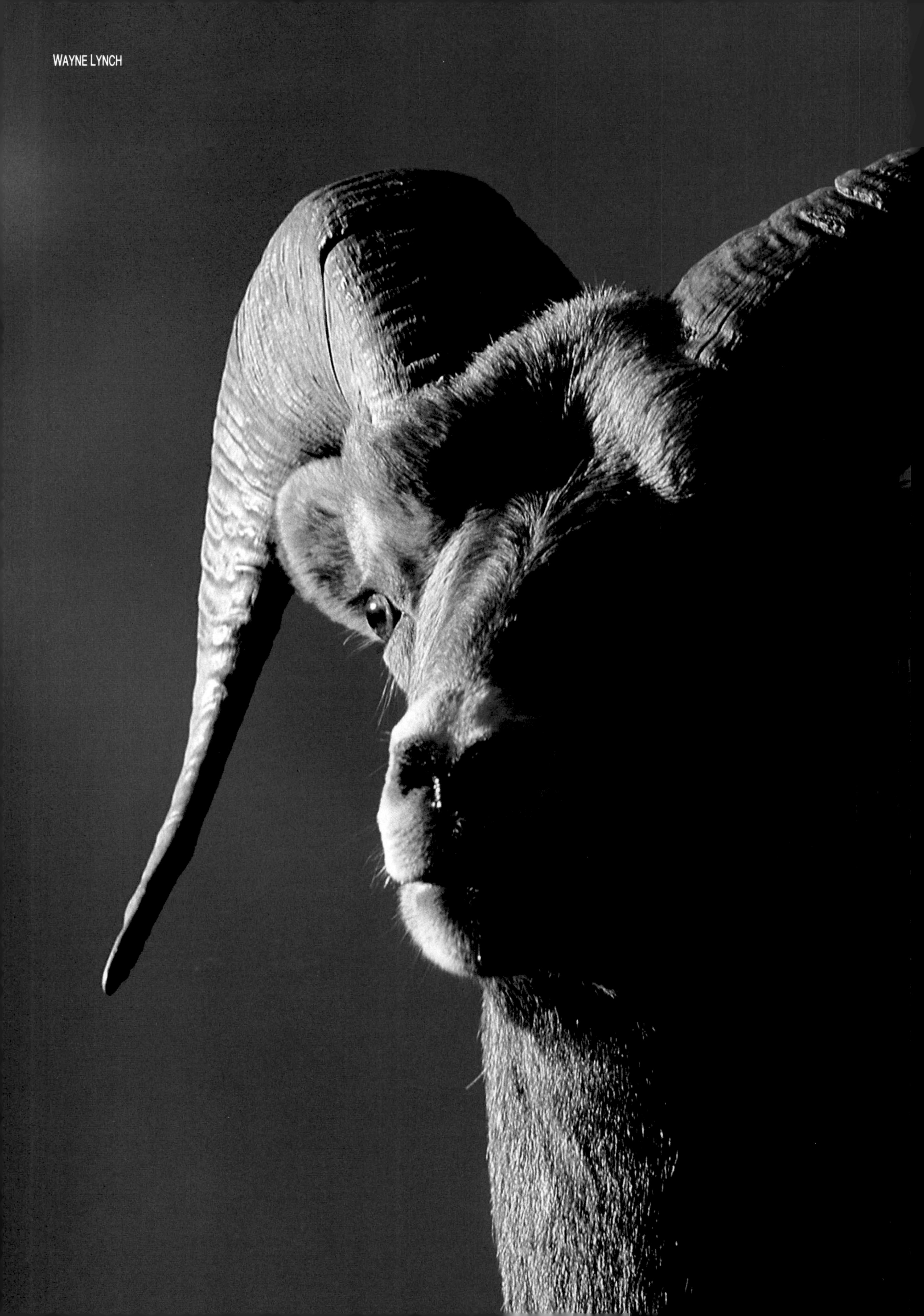

Wildlife is very important to me, and national surveys confirm that wildlife is important to most Canadians. Every year over 80% of the population participates in a wildlife-related activity. We read books and magazines about wildlife, we watch it on television and in films, we observe it in zoos, aquariums, parks and museums, we protect it and feed it around our homes, and a million of us are members in organizations that believe in its intrinsic worth and the contribution it makes to the quality of life.

WAYNE LYNCH

WAYNE WEGNER

WAYNE WEGNER

WAYNE LYNCH

JERRY CLEMENT

Wildlife inspires our poets, fuels our writers, and challenges our photographers and painters. In early times, wildlife was inextricably woven into the lives of men. Today, although most of us live in forests of steel and glass, far removed from other creatures, we continue to be drawn to wildlife and wildlife remains an integral part of our emotional fabric.

PETER HOLTON

WAYNE LYNCH

KEITH LOGAN

DOUG LEIGHTON

That wildlife interests us is easy to determine but hard to explain. It may be that we are attracted to its esthetic qualities, for wildlife often embodies beauty, grace and strength. Or it may be that we are naturally drawn to anything alive, and are refreshed by viewing other forms of life. Or is it that we envy its freedom, saddled as we are with the trappings of culture? Or it may simply be that we crave simplicity once more, because for wildlife, there is no right or wrong, good or bad, only life and death.

WAYNE LYNCH

GERARD YUNKER

PRAIRIES
A LAND FOR TOMORROW

Prairies
A LAND FOR TOMORROW

It doesn't matter what emotion I feel, when I am on the prairies, the feeling is more intense. On the prairies when I am happy, I feel playful and young and I have often had the urge to chase a tumble-weed. And, on the prairies when the meadowlarks sing and the summer sun enhances the fragrance of my lover's hair, that is when I feel most loving.

ROBERTO DE LUNA

Hudson's Bay Company.

INCORPORATED 2ND MAY 1670.

TED ZAWASKI

The Blackfoot, Cree, Piegan and Blood Indians were the first to call the prairies home. Theirs was the time of the buffalo when bawling herds stretched to the horizon, and the people moved with the animals and danced to the sun. After the downfall of Louis Riel in Manitoba, in 1870, small groups of Metis moved to the prairies to hunt the buffalo, but the herds were already dwindling and the end was near. The West was wild then, and "whiskey" forts fueled the tempers of lawless men. As a remedy the Northwest Mounted Police were established in 1874 and the "red coats" soon brought order to the land.

CARLOS AMAT

WAYNE LYNCH

DOUG LEIGHTON

ANTHONY CHODAS

LARRY FISHER

168

AL KATOWITZ

By the 1880's the buffalo were gone from the prairies and it was the golden age of ranching. The ranches were big, the T-Bar-Down, Lazy S, and "76" Ranch, and the cowboys were tougher than the weather. Bustling cow towns sprouted along the newly laid railway. But the railway brought another change, it brought settlers from the East.

Between 1900-1920 the "sodbusters" poured into the prairies to plow the soil and tame the land. But soon the cattlemen and the farmers would learn that on the prairies, you can bully the land but you can never beat it. The winter of 1906-1907 brought the ranchers to their knees and cattle died by the thousands.

AL TAMBOSSO

DAN WALKER

MARK VITARIS

RON SCHWENGER

Throughout this time though, the cattlemen kept their clout and it wasn't until the oil boom of the 1970's that the boys with the beef finally stepped down from the saddle and passed the reins to the oilmen who still hold the power. Today, the prairies are still a patchwork of ranches and farms, the larder of our land.

Now the tenants walk more gently and live from day to day. They have learned that no one owns the prairies.

PATRICK PARENTEAU

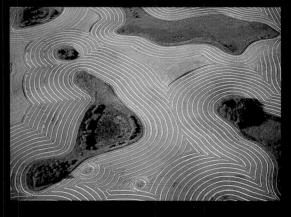

175

MARK VITARIS

RON SCHWENGER

RON SCHWENGER

AL TAMBOSSO

PATRICK PARENTEAU

PAT PRICE

179

OIL & GAS
THE POWER BENEATH

AL PALOMBO

It is said that "oil is found in the minds of men", for even today with the aid of topographical maps and aerial photographs, magnetometers and seismographs, the final decision to drill for oil often rests on an oilman's hunch. Oilmen and their industry are the substance of legends – sweat and grime under wild prairie skies, unbending rock and granite-willed men, and overnight fortunes earned and lost.

ROBERTO DE LUNA

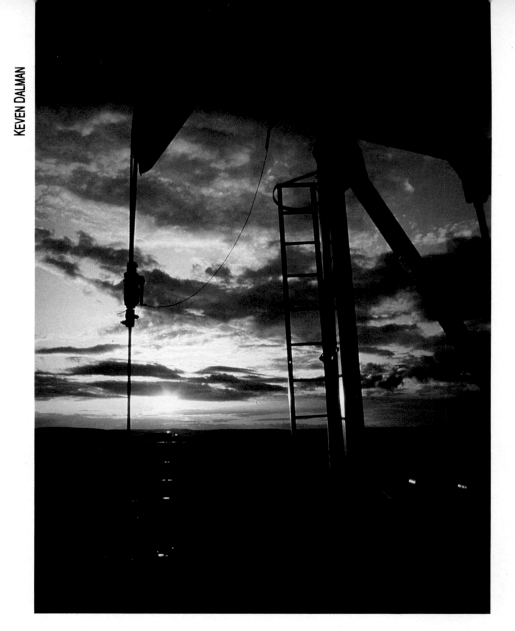

KEVEN DALMAN

AL PALOMBO

Oil is a fossil fuel derived from ancient seas. Then, organisms (plankton and algae) died and piled up on the ocean floor. At the same time the organisms mixed with rock sediments which were also accumulating. Over great spans of time two things occurred: The dead organisms decomposed into oil and the sediments were compressed into rocks, trapping the oil. Millions of years later, men tapped these rocks and pumped out the power as petroleum.

Petroleum is the major energy source for Canada, and Alberta produces the lion's share of our nation's needs. It was first discovered in the province near Calgary in 1910, and since the 1950's the region's destiny has been coupled with crude. Today, royalties from the petroleum industry keep the province's coffers full and makes "blue-eyed shieks" of elected men.

HOWARD CHURCH

185

GERARD YUNKER

XV Olympic Winter Games
Calgary/Canada

SHARE THE FLAME

A LONG ROAD HOME

CANADA
DETERMINATION & PRIDE

SHARE THE FLAME
A LONG ROAD HOME

GERARD YUNKER

The sponsor, Petro-Canada, calls it "the biggest Olympic event" – an 88 day odyssey that covers 18,000 kilometers and involves more than 6,500 participants. The event is the torch relay which brings the flame, and the Olympic spirit, from Greece on the shores of the Mediterranean, to Calgary in the foothills of the Canadian Rocky Mountains. The relay occurs in the middle of winter and traverses some of the coldest, most remote regions of the country, a tribute to the fortitude, determination and pride of the Canadian people.

PETRO-CANADA AND BAKER LOVICK

PETRO-CANADA AND BAKER LOVICK

As with the sporting events, the tradition of the torch originated with the ancient Greeks. In Olympia, a special shrine held glowing embers dedicated to the goddess Hestia. Every four years athletes would fan the embers into flames and then compete in "torch races". In the history of the modern Olympics, ceremonial ignition of the Olympic flame was first performed in Amsterdam in 1928. When the flame is lit for the XV Olympic Winter Games in Calgary on February 13, 1988 the torch relay will have been the longest in the history of the event.

The historic torch relay begins in Olympia, where the flame was ignited by the rays of the sun. The torch, designed to resemble the Calgary Tower, was then flown by Canadian Airlines International to start its nationwide journey in St. John's Newfoundland on November 17, 1987. Carried high by energetic Canadians, the torch proceeded at 125 kilometers a day, reaching Ontario by mid December and Saskatchewan a month later.

GERARD YUNKER

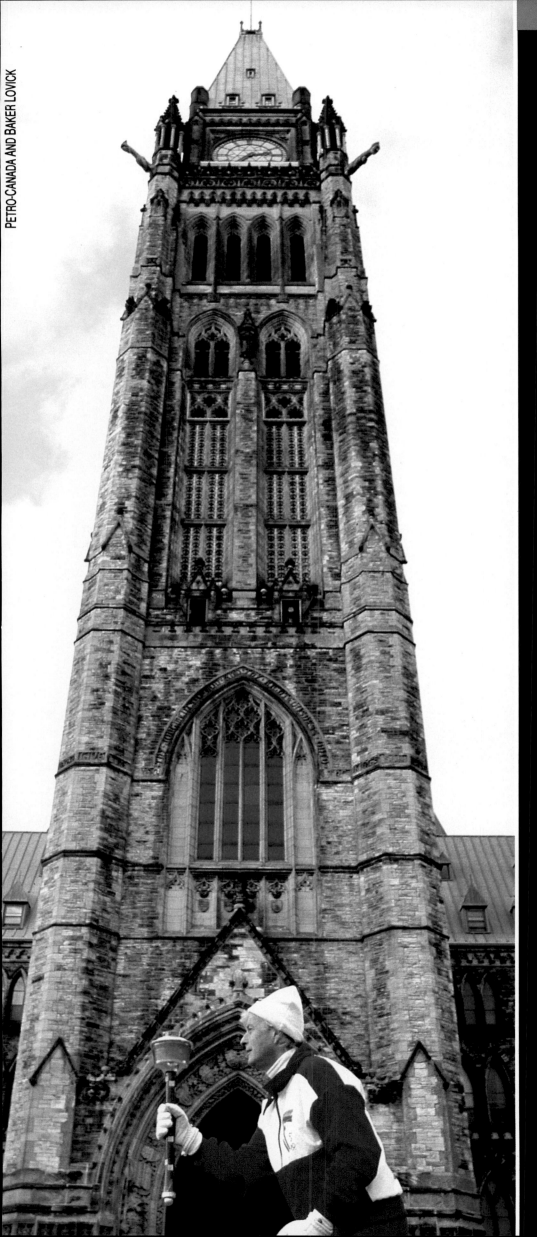

Once in Saskatchewan the relay changed course and travelled north by plane to Yellowknife and then on to the Inuit community of Inuvik. This is the first time that the flame has crossed the Arctic Circle. From Inuvik the torch journeys south to British Columbia and then makes a final circuit in Alberta arriving in time for the opening ceremonies in Calgary on February 13. The torch will have visited every capital city and every other major city in the country, and the flame will have passed within distance of 65% of Canada's population.

The real story of the torch relay, however, is the stories of the ordinary Canadians whose vitality and vision make this country the great nation that that it is.

The last time that Canadians carried the Olympic torch was in Montreal in 1976. Then, two strangers, a young man from Montreal and a young woman from Toronto, representing our bilingual heritage, ignited the Olympic flame. The strangers later became man and wife. The 1988 Olympic Winter Games may not ignite a romance, but it will fuel the flames of Canadian identity.

LARRY FISHER

195

GEORGE BRYBYCIN

MIKE RYAN

ROYAL BANK

FOCUS
THE F-STOPS HERE

The challenge was to document the making of an Olympic host city.

The task was enormous and required 80 photographers to dedicate one full year (709,560-man hours) of their lives to produce over 100,000 images from 3000 rolls of film. Only 300 of the best photographs were selected from the 4 kilometers (2.5 miles) of celluloid processed during the year. 750 hours of colour separation and stripping time were required prior to 908 kilograms (2008 pounds) of ink being applied onto 36.3 metric tonnes (80,000 pounds) of paper.

The result is Calgary - A Year In Focus.

The Year In Focus team used Kodak products exclusively throughout this publication, from photography, colour separations, to printing plates. Calgary - A Year In Focus is the first major publication to feature results from the new 64 ASA, 120mm and 200 ASA 35mm Kodachrome professional films. Kodak paper was used in the Linotronic 300 laser imagesetter and for all print reproductions.

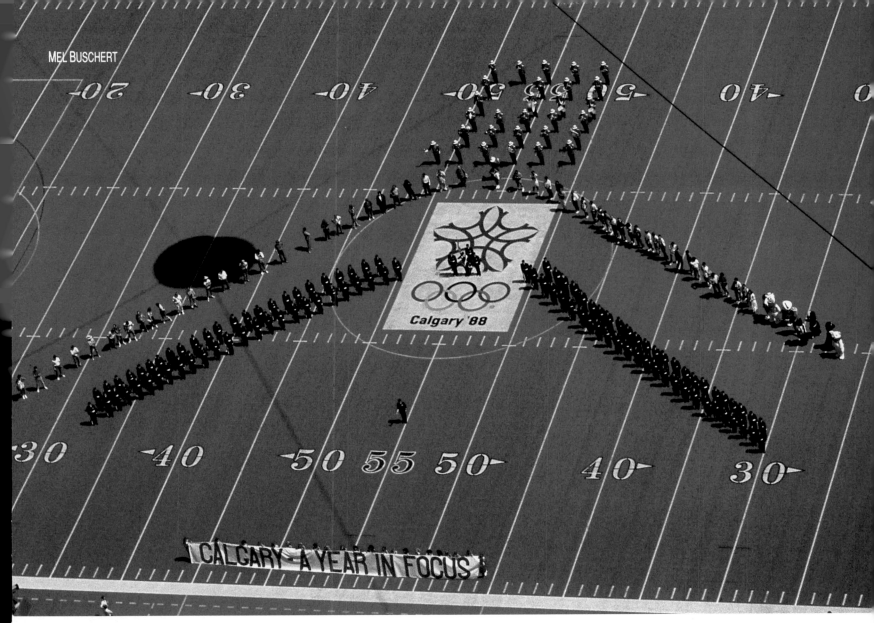

MEL BUSCHERT

CALGARY - A YEAR IN FOCUS

DOUG BROWN

PHOTOGRAPHERS

1 CARLOS AMAT
Born in Lisbon, Portugal, Carlos moved to Calgary in 1966. He attended Bishop Grandon high school before going to Mt. Royal College. After taking 2 years of police sciences, he moved to Ontario and worked for 3 years on the provincial government Tac-Team. He returned to Calgary in 1983 to become a staff photographer with the Calgary Sun. Carlos is 28 and single.

2 ELLIS BARTKIEWICZ
Ellis is a Calgary photographer who graduated with a BFA from the University of Calgary in 1978. Ellis runs an individual / independent free-lance photographic business that specializes in artists portfolios, portraits, and industrial work. She operates her own darkroom facility to control product through to completion.

3 JOHN BICKNELL
John Bicknell likes to combine the elements of nature and photography to "paint" pictures that can not be normally seen by the naked eye. Special thanks to CALGARY - A YEAR IN FOCUS for my first ever exhibition of pictures published. John's company is "BEYOND THE LENS IMAGES". 403 249-3724

4 HANK BOERE
Hank was a late bloomer who didn't take his photography seriously until he was over 40. Today there is nothing he would rather do than get lost in the foothills around Calgary with his camera. Hank may be contacted at 403 288-6339.

5 MEL BUSCHERT
Mel Buschert is an accomplished Photographer, Author and Technician displaying constant innovation and technical ability. The unique combination of Graphic Arts and photographic skills have proved valuable to many clients in Canada and the United States. Through extensive training, as a Kodak representative, he now designs and produces projects for High Country Colour, an award winning publisher and Official Licensee for the 1988 Olympic Winter Games.

6 BARBARA BRANDER
Barbara was born in Calgary. She graduated from the Alberta College of Art in 1978. She majored in a four year program in photographic arts and specializes in photo journalism, fashion, and fine art. She is a free-lance photographer and can be reached at 403 936-5729.

7 DOUG BROWN
Doug used a vintage 360 degree camera to obtain the Big Shot on pages 202-203.

8 GEORGE BRYBYCIN
George Brybycin is a renowned and passionate photographer, daring mountaineer, devoted naturalist and active publisher. He is the author of 12 pictorial publications. Conqueror of over 300 mountains in the Canadian Rockies. His photographs have been published in Europe the USA and Canada. George is currently working on a new book titled "ROMANCE OF THE ROCKIES" depicting his lifelong affair with these mountains.

9 GARY CAMPBELL
Originally from Montreal, Campbell specializes in fashion and commercial stills. A self taught photographer, he learned by "doing the work". Trained as a commercial pilot, he has travelled, lived, and photographed in many remote areas of the world, including two years in South America. He now owns and operates High Light Studios in Calgary, working with his colleague, Ian Tomlinson. Campbell also shoots for U.S. agencies including, The Chicago Models Group, Paulines, and the American Models of New York. 403 233-2575

10 DAVID CAROL
David came to us from New York City to cover the 1986 Calgary Exhibition and Stampede.

11 JIM CARROLL
A Montreal native who has made Calgary his home for many moons. He likes the Flames, but will die with his HAB's sweater on. Jim still studies photography at the " hard knox academy " and while forever seeking that perfect shot, supplements the passion with photographic instruction and consultation services through SPECTRUM INSTRUCTION 403 276-9061.

12 DAVE CHIDLEY
My interest in photography began in Toronto when I worked on the high school paper and yearbook. I started my professional career as a photographer with the Toronto Sun after graduation from the photography department at Ryerson Polytechnical Institute. I moved to Calgary five years ago to work as a staff photographer with the Calgary Sun. It was here that I met my wife Doreen and became a proud father.

13 ANTHONY CHODAS
Trained as a Design Engineer, Anthony enjoys both the technical and artistic sides of photography that come together when making an image. The entire photographic process fascinates him; from the pre-visualization stage to the final transparency, a 2 square inch depiction of reality. This truly is magic!!!

14 HOWARD CHURCH
Howard was born in England and emigrated to Canada in 1947. He is now a retired real estate broker who teaches adult classes in basic photography and darkroom techniques. He has won numerous photo awards and has contributed sports, architectural and oil industry photos to various magazines and newspapers.

15 JERRY CLEMENT
Jerry is a free-lance photographer who shoots to preserve images of momentary changes in life for himself and others. Jerry has had memorable success in his photographic work and has had his images reproduced in numerous publications and calendars. He will continue to strive to create the perfect image through the lens of his camera.

16 RENE CONLIN
Rene was born in the Badlands and raised as a coal miner's daughter. Her family moved to Calgary when she was nine because of a lack of coal. Rene first discovered her photographic talent at SAIT where she studied for two years in the Journalism Arts Program before graduating with a Diploma of Applied Arts. She is currently employed in the editorial department of the Calgary Herald where she aspires to become a Photojournalist.

17 DAVID CORRY
David was born in Ontario but is now a resident of Calgary. David uses his rural background and contemporary style to express a personal perspective in the landscapes and scenic images he captures. He is an owner of JAY DEE MEDIA and produces audio visual programs, wall decor, and wall portraiture. David is a principle of A Year In Focus productions and has worked hard for the success of this publication. He wishes to thank every one who participated.

18 DOUGLAS CURRAN
Doug is best known for his extended documentary projects, ranging from the Metis of Alberta, to UFO cultists, and travelling tent preachers in the southern USA. He is the author / photographer of "In Advance of the landing": Folk concepts of Outer Space. Doug works commercially as an architectural photographer and as a stillsman for the motion picture industry.

19 KEVEN DALMAN
Keven was raised in the midwest before moving to Vancouver in 1983. He has been shooting professionally since 1986.

20 ANDRAS DANCS
From the steaming jungles of Mexico to the frozen wastes of Canada's high arctic, Vancouver based annual report, editorial and stock photographer Andras Dancs has been there. The recipient of a New York Art Directors Club 1987 Award for colour editorial photography, Dancs work can also be seen in Applied Arts, Photographies, and the National Archives of Canada.

21 DAC DANG
Dac Dang took up photography fifteen years ago and used it as a therapeutic diversion from his Ph. D. studies in engineering. Photography still offers therapy from his instructors job at Mount Royal College. His works cover all angles of photography. Dac specializes in exhibitional works in museums and galleries.

22 STEVE DARBY
Steve Darby is a free-lance photographer currently involved in photojournalism and sports assignments. He also teaches photography at the high school level. Steve is a graduate of the Pacific Academy of Photography and resides in Calgary.

23 ROBERTO DE LUNA
Roberto is particularly interested in industrial and audio-visual photography. While living in Mexico City in 1974, he graduated in Cinematography studies. He then moved to France to study Visual Arts at La Sorbonne University. Roberto won the Luis Bunuel grant for the best photography in the film "Partir de Cero" His clients include: Husky Oil, Pan Canadian, Minolta, and the Mexican subsidiaries of : Ford, Nestle, Uniroyal, Burroughs and Pemex. 403 282-8238

24 MICHAEL DREW
Michael was born in Chilliwack B.C., but has lived in Southern Alberta since he was 6 months old. He is a self taught photographer that apprenticed with the fine photographers at the Lethbridge Herald. "I enjoy photographing life in all forms, but especially things that are uniquely Western. I would like to thank my small hairy companion, Ausey, for his continued support and friendship."

25 TINO DUSOSWA
Tinos creative eyes have just begun to see.

26
PHILIP DYKES

Philip was born and raised in Calgary. He has had a long standing interest in the visual arts and has attended the Alberta College of Art, Photographic Arts program, 1982 - 1985. Philip has continued his education as a photographic assistant for such names as BOLLI & HUTCHINSON PHOTOGRAPHIC DESIGN, GERARD YUNKER, and Toronto firms BENTLEY, SHARPSHOOTER, and ART AND DESIGN STUDIOS. His goal is to be a versatile, world class shooter.

27
TOM ERICSON

I am a sports photographer specializing in ski photography. I live for skiing and love to ski. Photography was always a hobby for me. But after working as a ski model for a couple of years, I saw the opportunity to expand my hobby into a profession that I could really enjoy. Working on this project was a good chance for me to gain exposure in something other than sports photography. 403 252-3277

28
LARRY FISHER

Larry Fisher specializes in Aerial, Advertising, Commercial, Editorial, Industrial, and Illustrative photography. Mr. Fisher is an Official photographer to the 1988 Olympic Winter Games. His clients include ABC, Alberta and Federal Governments, Chatelaine, City of Calgary, Coca-Cola, CTV, General Motors, International Olympic Committee, Labatts, Motorola, Royal Lepage, Visa, Sports Illustrated, Time, Sun Ice. He is experienced in European and Asian location photography.

29
DAN FREEMAN

Dan is a well known D.J. in Calgary and finds photography to be another form of creative expression.

30
JOHN FUJIMAGARI

John was born and raised in Alberta. Photography has been his passion since grade school. He has studied with John Shaw and Courtney Milne and has been published in National Geographic. John spends most of his time travelling and specializes in outdoor photography. 403 248-3197

31
DALE HANNAFORD

Dale was born in Calgary in 1950 and graduated from the Alberta College of Art in 1975. He studied Fine Art Painting for 4 years and then worked as a co-ordinator of advertising and promotions for the next three years. Dale and his wife travelled extensively throughout Africa before returning to Calgary to work as a free-lance industrial photographer. Dale is happily married and has two children.

32
PETER HOLTON

Peter was born in England in 1940 and moved to Canada in 1974. He worked in Toronto for three years before moving to Calgary in 1977. A draftsman by trade, Peter turned to his favorite hobby, photography, when the recession hit Alberta in 1982.

33
KEVIN JOHNSTON

Kevin's hometown is Cobalt, Ontario. He studied photography at Confederation College in Thunder Bay, Ontario, from 1983 - 1986. He has lived in Calgary for the past year and is employed at CFB Calgary. He is working towards a career in stock photography. 403 246-3145

34
INGO KALK

Ingo was born in West Berlin, Germany. He lived in Calgary since 1960 before moving to Canmore in time to enjoy the 1988 Olympic Winter Games. He is currently seeking a Fine Arts Degree at the University of Calgary. Ingo is a free-lance nature and people photographer who took his first photograph in 1954.

35
ALAN KATOWITZ

Alan was born in Cleveland, Ohio on April 25, 1947. He lived in San Francisco before moving to Vancouver, B.C. He spent four years in the Queen Charlotte Islands where he established Queen Charlotte Photo services and specialized in resource, landscape and people photography. His expertise in commercial, architectural, and performing Arts work has earned him respect in the photographic industry. Available for assignments world wide. 604 667-9232   305 947-6147

36
ERIC KLUS

Eric lived in Montreal, Quebec before moving to the White Rock, B.C. in 1984. Eric is a serious traveller who uses his photography to document the world around him. His first visit to the city of Calgary and the surrounding badlands forever changed his opinion of the Canadian Midwest, and he now plans to continue pursuing this newly found interest.

37
EDMOND H. KOELLE

Ed was born and raised in Calgary! He began his photography career in 1979. He is now a member of the Alberta Professional Photographers Association and was elected president of the Calgary Photographic Society in 1987. Ed offers a variety of photographic services including: aerial, commercial, industrial, illustration, public relations and portraiture. Contact: PHANTOM PHOTOGRAPHY 403 285-7669

38
LANCE KJERSTEEN

Lance is a 24 year old native of Calgary who studied photography in junior high school. He studied photojournalism while enrolled in the Journalism Arts program at SAIT. Lance worked as the photo editor at the Emery Weal newspaper at SAIT before his current position as the sports editor at the High River Times.

39
DOUGLAS LEIGHTON

As a native of Banff, Doug is strategically located to photograph Canadian landscapes, nature, culture, commerce and recreation. He has been published in Canadian Geographic, CDN Nature Federation, National Audubon Society, National Geographic Society, Time Life Books, and exhibits internationally through External Affairs and Nikon's Motion: A Celebration of Canada He also turns his camera to advertising and commercial purposes. 403 762-2248

40
KEITH LOGAN

Keith Logan specializes in photographing the natural environment using a large format camera. Even though his photographs have been published in National Geographic, Sierra Club and Nature Canada, his main focus is in the making of high quality colour prints. These prints are in the permanent collections of the Alberta Art Foundation, the Edmonton Art Gallery and the Whyte Museum of the Canadian Rockies. 403 932-3232

41
WAYNE LYNCH

Wayne Lynch is a top professional wildlife and nature photographer whose photographs have been published in a dozen countries, and such eminent North American societies as the National Geographic, Audubon, Sierra Club and the National Wildlife Federation. Wayne is also the author for Calgary-A Year in Focus.

42
VALERIE MANTYKA

Valerie specializes in fashion, location and advertising photography in Calgary. Valerie is a recent graduate from the Alberta College of Arts, Photographic Arts program. Her motto: Fresh images, Fresh ideas.

43
LARRY MARTINI

Larry is a plant supervisor for Canada Lafarge in Calgary. He and his wife, Jackie have three boys, Jesse, Christopher, and Joel. Larry worked on this project because he wanted to make a contribution to such a fine book, and to a great city.

44
STUART McCALL

At nineteen years of age Stuart McCall took to the road at the beginning of an exciting career of photography and travel. For the past eight years he has been based in Vancouver, Canada, where he is a principal of North Light Images.. Stuart continues to travel extensively, specializing in annual report, editorial, and stock photography.

45
RAY McNEIL

After graduating from the School of Modern Photography in Montreal, Quebec, Ray slowly worked his way west to discover that Calgary and the Rocky Mountains are enough to challenge the creativity of any photographer.

46
KEN A. MEISNER

Ken became interested in photography at an early age as he watched his father take the family travel pictures while visiting Europe and North America. He bought his first camera, a 35mm SLR in 1974. Ken's unique perspective and photographic vision can best be described as "painting with light." He would like to thank CAYIF for the opportunity to shoot for them.

47
MARK MENNIE

Mark is a fourth year photography student at the Alberta College of Art. He began his career working for the Chestermere High school yearbook. He has trained as a photographic assistant and will work as a professional after graduation. "Special thanks to Mr Derek Rawlinson, my high school photography instructor for his constant encouragement, thus allowing me to pursue my dream."

48
ALAN MERRETT

Alan is the owner / operator of FX Photographic Artwork Inc., Calgary, Alberta. He attended SAIT and studied in the Advertising Sales Division. Alan specializes in the field of abstract images and custom darkroom techniques. Alan says of his work, "I believe the use of un-orthodox ideas is essential to create unique, new effects". 403 249-0177

49
LES MESZAROS

Les Meszaros has a B.Sc. in Geography from the University of Calgary. He is an active naturalist and concentrates his photography in the areas of wildlife and landscapes. He worked for several years in environmental planning before working at KLM Royal Dutch Airlines. Les is married and is celebrating the recent addition of a son and small mad dog to the family.

50
JIM MILLER

Jim Miller hails from Calgary's sister and rival city from the north, Edmonton. He struggled for 13 years to obtain an education degree in Art and Design at the University of Calgary. He worked on the U of C Gazette for the next four years as a writer / photographer. In the fall of 1987, Jim began a new challenge as an instructor of Journalism at the Grant MacEwan Community College in Edmonton. He enjoys writing, painting and of course, Photography.

51
BRAD MOORE

Brad, 24 is a major in Photographic Arts at the Alberta College of Art in Calgary. He enjoys photographing sports, people and landscapes and will pursue a career in journalism or commercial photography. Brad feels that he has gained valuable experience shooting for Calgary-A Year In Focus.

52
DAVID OLECKO

David was born in Edmonton, Alberta on Sept. 16, 1960. He attended elementary and Jr. high schools in Calgary. David studied Public Relations and Photojournalism at Mount Royal College. He worked at the Calgary Herald in 1984 as part of a summer internship before obtaining his current position as a photographer with the Calgary Sun in 1985.

53
BRUCE OTJES

Bruce is a free-lance photographer with a creative instinct developed over the years. He interests are varied, and he rises to the challenge to make each picture better than the last. Bruce knows the joys of getting a great shot.

54
AL PALOMBO

Al has been an active photojournalist and industrial photographer operating out of Calgary. When not on assignment, he works on expanding his photo stock library of Alberta material. He would like to thank Birnie of Appletree Photographic for his assistance. 403 244-6442

55
PATRICK PARENTEAU

Mr. Parenteau is the president of I-MEDIA productions Ltd.in Vancouver, B.C., a company that specializes in Audio Visual production and photographic marketing. Patrick is the executive producer and photo editor for Calgary-A Year In Focus. "I would like to congratulate all of our photographers for making the Calgary-A Year In Focus publication 'A WORK OF ART' and not just another picture book."

PHOTOGRAPHERS

▶ 56
DAVE PARKER
Dave is a free-lance photographer working in and around the Calgary area developing his image bank of mountain and prairie landscapes. He enjoys industrial and commercial work, but favours sports photography from skydiving to underwater assignments with the Aquabelles. He would like to thank "Debbie Muir and Carolyn Waldo for their great patience with me underwater." David was educated at Humber College in Toronto. 403 238-0771

▶ 57
BRUCE PICKERING
Bruce has worked as a professional photographer since 1972. After completing his B.Sc. at the University of Wisconsin, he returned to Canada to commence his career as a livestock portrait photographer, specializing in dairy cattle. Bruce and his family settled in Calgary in 1982. Hot air ballooning is a favorite hobby.

▶ 58
PATRICK PRICE
Patrick has been a local photojournalist for the past six years. He works as a stringer for REUTERS and has covered every major event in Alberta, from Stanley Cups, to Olympic Preview events. When he is not on assignment, Patrick pursues his favorite vocation and hobby PHOTOGRAPHY.

▶ 59
DAVID PULLAR
David is a free-lance photographer and native Calgarian. He specializes in editorial and commercial photography but has a particular interest in world cup and national sporting events. David will graduate from the U of C with a B.Comm.

▶ 60
MIKE RIDEWOOD
Mike Ridewood got his start in photography working with the Canadian Press in Ottawa. Mike's major clients include Canadian Pacific, Maclean's Magazine Reuters and Foothills Hospital. He specializes in sports and commercial photography and covers most major events in Alberta.

▶ 61
DANNY RIEDLHUBER
Danny Riedlhuber worked as a photojournalist at the Lethbridge Herald in May 1979. He has been working as a photographer at the Calgary Sun since September 1984.

▶ 62
SCOTT ROWED
A Canadian rockies native, Scott Rowed is a full time professional photographer, specializing in skiing and action sports. His extensive photo credits include National Geographic, and the majority of B.C.'s supernatural winter ads. Phone Banff 403 762-3134.

▶ 63
RICK RUDNICKI
Without any intentional, fancy way of adjusting yourself, express yourself as you are.

▶ 64
MIKE RYAN
Mike received a B.A. in Sociology in 1976. Mike graduated from a four year program in Photographic Art in 1976. He is a free-lance photographer and specializes in commercial, photojournalism and sports.

▶ 65
RON SCHWENGER
Ron was born is Guelph, Ontario and moved to Vancouver to work for Air Canada. Ron's international travels inspired him to pursue a career in photography. He now works as an advertising marketing rep. and professional photographer who combines photographic excellence with creative design. Ron is currently in the process of moving his stock images from Masterfile and Westock, into an agency in Los Angeles. His loves are flying and son Dylan.

▶ 66
STEVEN SPEER
Steven specializes in colour and black and white landscape photography. He has been a professional photographer for the past 15 years and studied photography at the Alberta College of Art. He is currently employed as a Research Technician for Canadian Hunter Exploration Ltd. and spends weekends photographing in the mountains.

▶ 67
MITCH STRINGER
The more I photograph, the more I visualize unique images that need to be captured on film. A viscous cycle that offers me immeasurable pleasure. As a result, I formed my own photographic company, ECLIPSE IMAGES, that allows me to pursue a career in this very exciting field of work. 403 293-0812

▶ 68
ROY SULLIVAN
R. Roy Sullivan is a professional dilettante currently involved in extensive R + D in the area of advanced, thoughtful, conscientious hedonism and tasteless humor. His goals in life are to find the perfect Armagnac but not too soon and favorite trout stream, as soon as possible!

▶ 69
LLOYD SUTTON
Lloyd is a native of Vancouver who journeyed to Calgary to photograph Mayor Ralph Klein. He has many corporate clients that keep him travelling world wide. His favorite question, "Where is my Kodachrome?"

▶ 70
ALAN TAMBOSSO
Alan Tambosso is a 29 year old geologist who looks for oil for a living and shoots photography for fun. Alan was born in Richmond Hill, Ontario, but has been a Calgarian since 1981. He says, "Calgary is a GREAT city to live and work in. I am sure that Calgary-A Year In Focus will show this to the world".

▶ 71
ALEXANDER THOMAS
Alexander W. Thomas is a Calgary free-lance entertainment photographer and does both live and studio shots of local, national, and international acts. Alexander feature work includes everything from Rock and Roll to theater and ballet. His credits include publication in newspapers and magazines across Canada, and his photos have been used internationally on albums and for promotional use.

▶ 72
IAN TOMLINSON
Mr. Tomlinson specializes in outdoor sports photography. He has travelled extensively covering corporate and editorial clients. Ian operates HIGHLIGHT STUDIOS along with his colleague, Gary Campbell, and produces images for a variety of commercial applications. For details phone 403 233-2575

▶ 73
MARK VITARIS
Mark Vitaris is a photojournalist and audio visual producer. Mark is a native of Buffalo, New York, and graduated from the University of Ottawa before moving to Calgary in 1978. His portfolio includes annual and editorial photography, and multi image slide presentations for major corporations and associations. Maxim: 'THINK VISUAL !!'

▶ 74
DAN WALKER
Dan Walker is a free-lance outdoor, writer / photographer. He lives in the City of Calgary and writes for national hunting publications. Dan enjoys photographing wildlife, nature, and scenes that depict historic rural Alberta. Of his wildlife subjects, Dan says that the toughest animal to photograph is the mature Whitetail buck. 403 246-0669

▶ 75
GEORGE WEBBER
George Webber is a photographer and instructor at the Southern Alberta Institute of Technology. George's photographs reside in major collections of Canada, Germany, France and Australia. His work has been published in numerous photographic journals including, American Photographer, Camera Mainichi, Camera Canada, Canon Chronicle and Leica Fotografie.

▶ 76
WAYNE WEGNER
Free-lance, wildlife photographer Wayne Wegner, a native of Red Deer, Alberta, earned his bachelor's degree in environmental biology at the University of Windsor in Ontario. His travels in search of stunning nature images have taken him from the pacific coast of Vancouver Island to the eastern shores of Newfoundland.

▶ 77
ROGER WHEATE
Roger Wheate 35 has been a photographic technician and lecturer in the Geography department, University of Calgary, since 1981. His photography concentrates on physical and cultural landscapes, inspired by teaching courses in Geography since 1975, coupled with the diversity of environments in Western Canada. Roger has had a 20 year addiction to long distance running, which has proved to be a significant advantage in capturing more photographic images.

▶ 78
ROCK WHITNEY
Rock Whitney is a native Calgarian who is a free-lance pilot, film maker, and photographer. Rock specializes in people, adventure and high technology. His personal favorites are space shots and has covered a number of early space shuttle missions. 403 244-3471

▶ 79
GERARD YUNKER
BUSY, BUSY, BUSY!!! It's been one heck-uv a good time since I've graduated from the Alberta College of Art in 1986. TRAVEL, GLITTER, ROMANCE!!!....All in a days work! 50 words isn't nearly enough to accommodate my client list, so I'd just like to take this opportunity to thank each and everyone of you. SO THANXS!!!! 403 269-8345

▶ 80
TED ZAWASKI
Ted has been an avid photographer for the past 43 years and has worked in Canada, Europe and Morocco. He is a diversified photographer that has a special passion for macro wildlife work. Ted does his own colour and B+W printing, and is an active member of the Foothills Camera Club. 403 276-6954

ED KOELLE

"When I make that last, inevitable ride to the country up there where the grass grows lush, green and stirrup-high, and where the water runs cool, clear and deep, I trust that You, my final judge, will tell me that my entry fees are paid."

Corporate Acknowledgments – Friends & Advisors

ABC Television
Rick Giacalone
Mark Roth
ABL Photographic Techniques Ltd.
Peter Bolli
Action Magazine
Ingrid Epp
Brian Hinde
AGT
Linda Abercrombie
Alberta Ballet Co.
Alta. College Of Art
Alberta Tourism
Alpine Helicopters
Ted Jansen
Neil Warren
Apple Canada Inc.
Kim Berg
Glenn Boyd
Grant Kendall
James Spack
Astral Photo
Bachynski, McClintock, Knibbe
Carl McClintock
Baker Lovick Advertising
Braidwood, Mac-Kenzie, Brewer
Brad Addison
Marie Claire Baillie
Butchart Grey Consultants
Calgary Board of Education
Calgary Centre for Preforming Arts
Calgary Chamber of Commerce
Bruce Green
Calgary Exhibition & Stampede
Calgary Fire Dept.
Calgary Flames
Calgary Herald
Calgary Magazine
Calgary Stampeders
Calgary Stampeder Cheerleaders
Calgary Zoo
Canadian Airlines International
Rhys Eyton
Darrel G. Smith
J. Graham Mann
Jack C. Lawless
Nic Roggeman
Ruth Montgomery
Canadian Magazine
Michael Davies
Gabriele Scheruble
Canon Canada Inc.
Leo Robichaud
Mary Muldar

CBC Radio
Sharon Edwards
Val Boser
Central Eye Gallery
CFAC Television
Brenda Finley
Rick Copley
CFB Calgary
CFCN Television
Robin Lawless
Glenn Grice
66 CFR
CISS-AM
Roy Hennessy
Wayne Bryant
City Of Calgary
Mayor Ralph Klein
Rod Love
Bob Holmes
Sheila-Marie Cook
Marilyn Kaiser
Hartvig Lauridsen
Isobel Grayston
Rose Kolibaba
Diane Easton
Sheila Woolner
Andy Gibson
Bob Pearson
Karen Prather
Claudio's Restaurant Group
Al La Monica
Claude La Monica
Coca-Cola Canada
Brian Martin
Dale Boniface
Jeff Miller
Commonwealth Capital Corp.
Kenneth F. Brunning
CTV Television
Tom Wells
Toni Dixon
Peter Sisam
Dancers Studio W.
Deloitte Haskins & Sells
Gerald L. Burrows
Alan M. Scrivener
Keith Rolfe
Paul Trotter
Mike Lavery
Design Plus
Esso Resources Ltd
Kent O'Connor
Richard Jeffery
First Western Printing
The Staff
General Motors
Blair Upton
Glenbow Museum
G.T.O. Printing
Government of Alberta
Premier Don Getty
Norman A. Weiss

Bernard F. Campbell
A.F. (Chip) Collins
Graphic Developments Ltd.
David Hutchison
Harvie Andre MP
Roy D. Heale & Associates
Roy D. Heale
Mike Thomas
Hollyhock House Publishing
Bev McDonald
Ray Carlton
Home Oil
Fred Callaway
Nancy Matthews
IBM
Leslie Roberts
Jim Rolston
Ken Whitmire & Associates
Kodak Canada
Harry J. Reid
Peter Allan
Patricia Ennis
Antony E. Chodas
Ed L. Barry
Brad Thompson
Labatt Brewing Co.
Michael Buist
Doug Balfour
Jeff Timson
Lavalin Inc.
Art Smith
Enid Bradley
Ruth Gordon
Linotype Canada Limited
Brian Deakin
Jim English
Len Furlotte
Troy Naber
Lloyds Bank
Loomis Courier Service
Mackin-Mailey Advertising
Macintosh Business Centre
Michael J. Readwin
Barbara Barnett
Evelyn Kelly
Scott Barnett
Maclean Hunter Ltd.
Ronald Osborne
James K. Warrillow
Manuel Vasaari
Eileen Maier
Tony G. Cantalini
Masterfile
Steve Pigeon
McKim Advertising
Music 96
Kevin Nelson
Bob Brown
Nova Photo

Panasonic
Ed Cameron
Personal Best
Petro-Canada Inc.
Mike Komisar
Bob Foulkes
Sheila O'Brien
Judy Wish
Dan Reynolds
Sandy Hunter
Tom Eason
Prime Minister's Office
Brian Mulroney
Gordon Grant
Mark Phillips
Q-91
Mark Kennedy
E. Jack Allen
Re/Max Real Estate
Frank Shreenan
Rick Baker
Ernest Jilg
Robinson's Camera
Royal Bank
Samantha Demidivacious
Jim Ramsay
Sears Canada, Inc.
Rose Sullivan
Spirit of '88
Jack Tennant
Sprung Sports Wear
Carrie Sprung
Mark Bowman
Sun Ice
Sylvia Rempel
Janice Rempel
Evalina Schmidtki
T.G. Painting
The Calgary Sun
Lynne Munro
Lesley Annett
Jim Davies
Marcel Clouthier
Sunshine Girls
3M
Tim Hoffman
Jim Radford
Thrifty Canada
Marni McKitrick
Jamie McBean
Bill McNeice
Larry Chiaravelle
United Graphic Services Limited
Gary MacDonald
Ron Buors
Bob Fielder
Mike Brackley
Robert Turner
Jon Rozander
Paul Ward
Karen Makowski
Kimberly Morhalo
Wayne Prentice

Kathleen McDowall
Dale Bickford
Marlene Risdon
United News
John Hazelton
University Of Calgary
USA Today
Porter Binks
Venex Capital Corporation
Bob Black
Vidatron Communications
Craig Sawchuk
Village Park Inn
Western Corp. Business Centre
Helmuth Strobel
Westin Hotel
Arthur Oades
Doug McLeod
Michele Maskell
Leona Dureau
Fran MacKay
Winter West Magazine
Jane Arnell
Bill & Adele Bailey
Wade Baldwin
Carol Bartell
"Karen B."
Amin Bhatia
Suri Bhatia
Dean Bicknell
"The Big Woman"
Reine Blackman
Bradford Boudreau
Eyrle & Muriel Brooks
Carolyn Brooks
Harry Brooks
Janet Bruch
Mark Brunton
Joan & David Bulman-Fleming
Barbara & Joe Cardle
Dr. David & Liz Chambers
Cameron Clark
Susan Clark
Trevor & Pat Coates
Mark Coates
Paul Coates
Donald J. Colton
Stan & Rita Day
Michael & Sophie Day
John S. & Donalda Corry
Mary Corry
Jim Corry
Rob Corry
Cam & Lyn Cuthill
Eric Dahlberg
Christine Dahlberg
Rick Dalton

Tom & Suzie Davidson
Matthew Davidson
Don Davies
Jack Davis
Rick De Koning
Paul De Koning
Michelle Delisle
Susan Dewar
Janice Dewart
Jim Dinning (MLA)
Dwight & Chrissy Dionne
Tom Durant
Bruce & Jan Dynes
Don & Merle Ericson
The Jutras Family
Marianne Fedori
Mark Fellows
Greg Forzani
John Galt
Nick & Mary Gershon
The Glaspie Girls
Diane Glover
Zenon Goral
Mark Gorak
G.G. Goulet
Catherine Goulet
Laura Goulet
Murray Goulet
Terry & George Goulet
Roger E. Grant
Belinda Grootveld
Rob Hadlow
Patricia Hargrave
Ian Hargrave
Ray Harris
Gene, Judy & Marci Hattori
Louise Hay
Suzanne Haymer
Charlene Hellson
Elaine Hiller
Greg Holmgren
Edna Howdle
Catherine Howe
Kathryn Hummel
Connie Hunt
Mark & Pat Hunter
Jason Jahrig
Oddette Jobidon
Cinnamon Johnston
Judy Johnston
John and Adele
Amber, Jamie & Kelly
Mark Kennedy
Ralph & Colleen Klein
Mr. & Mrs. Frank Klus
Sandy & Eric Klus
Ian Knight
Aubrey Lang
Dean & Carol Lailey
Trevor Lantz

Troy Lantz
Dick Le Blanc
Boyd Leader
Vance Letcher
Laura Lind
Matts Lindgren
B. Deane Little
Randy Lynde
Barry MacDonnell
Lynn Machan-Gorhan
Rob MacNiven
Kee Mah
Douglas Marshall
Conrad McElhaw
Sandy McLachlain
Dean McLean
Owen J. McGuire
Del Michaud
Keith Mills
Kim Moller
Jim Morphy
Kevin Nelson
Dora & Don Newman
"Oscar"
Rory O'Shea
"Pallapa"
Ernie & Marmie Parenteau
Ian & Sonja Parenteau
John Parker
David Perlman
Ty Reynolds
Murray Rothbard
David Lee Rust
Tony Sabo
Michael Shah
Steve Shaw
Doug Sissons
Anne Marie Slater
Michael Smith
Todd Smith
Chris Speare
Richard Standen
Miguel Stevens
Patty & Mike Tanner
Judy Teare
Mike Thomas
Erick Thompson
John & Marsha Van Esch
John Van Roessel
Ken Vance
Carolyn Waldo
Roy Wand (RCMP)
"Wardo"
Mr. George Webber
Mrs. Delphine Webber
Zenon West
Julie White
Joanne & Kristina White
Carrol Ann Williamson
Debbie Wilshire

ERIC KLUS